DIVORCES, SEPARATIONS AND ANNULMENTS IN MISSOURI

1769 TO 1850

Teresa Blattner

HERITAGE BOOKS
2024

HERITAGE BOOKS

AN IMPRINT OF HERITAGE BOOKS, INC.

Books, CDs, and more—Worldwide

For our listing of thousands of titles see our website
at
www.HeritageBooks.com

A Facsimile Reprint
Published 2024 by
HERITAGE BOOKS, INC.
Publishing Division
5810 Ruatan Street
Berwyn Heights, MD 20740

International Standard Book Number
Paperbound: 978-1-55613-695-5

DEDICATION

My great-grandpa used to tell me stories of his younger years, his family, and the people he knew. Grandpa's stories laid the foundation for both my love of history and genealogy. I dedicate this work to him, Guilford F. Zumwalt, 1886-1979.

TABLE OF CONTENTS

PREFACE

Laws governing the circumstances under which an injured party could file for a separation or divorce have varied considerably over the years. Under both Spanish and French rule, a divorce was unheard of. The only solution for an unhappy couple was a legal separation.

After the United States purchased the Louisiana Territory in 1803, the injured party in a marital dispute could petition for a divorce by proving adultery, desertion, or that their spouse had been a habitual drunkard for more than two years.

This compilation of early Missouri divorces and separations includes notices and information from territorial, state, and county newspapers. Early newspaper notices often noted the date, followed by "inst.", which stood for "instant", and referred to the current month. When a date was followed by the term "ult", it represented the previous month.

A commonly used phrase when a divorce petition was filed was "next friend". This term was used in reference to the person who appeared in court with the petitioner.

This work was compiled in the hope it will aid family researchers find the answer to missing spouses, or find a reason for large gaps in ages for the children of a couple. In my own family research, finding the divorce of Abraham Zumwalt and Juliet Hope answered many questions. I hope this work will do the same for someone else.

Teresa Blattner

ACKNOWLEDGEMENTS

I would like to thank the staff of the Callaway County Library, the Missouri State Archives, and the Historical Society of Missouri-Columbia. Most of all I want to thank Clark, Carrie, and Bethany for all their support, and for the many hours of watching TV over the clacking of the typewriter without complaint. Thanks guys!

RECORDS FROM LOWER COURT CASES,
1769 - 1845

Charles VALLE vs Pelegie CARPENTER- Divorce proceedings were begun in 1769, but Charles later dropped this petition. He again filed in the Ste. Genevieve Superior Court in 1783, but that petition was denied.

Louis COURTOIS vs Genevieve HUNAUD- This petition for a legal separation, was filed in Ste. Genevieve Superior Court in 1770, but was denied.

Louise LABROSSE vs Marie LANGEVIN- In 1778, this separation petition was submitted to the Ste. Genevieve Superior Court and approved the same year.

Pierre Francois REGNIER vs Louise Fellicite VALLE- When this petition for a legal separation was filed in 1812, in Ste. Genevieve Superior Court, it noted the couple had been married July 27, 1802, in St. Domingo. In his petition, Pierre asked for immediate custody of his two sons, Adolphus, and Alfred, and for custody of his daughter, Adele, when she turned five. Louise was to receive ten dollars per month for child support, and the use of a slave named Lisa.

Sally HANNAH, by her next friend, Isaac MEORLEY vs Enos HANNAH- This petition was filed during the May term 1812, in Ste. Genevieve Superior Court, and continued to the October term. It was dismissed when the Court learned Enos had died.

Mary GAINES, by her next friend, John M. HINKS vs James GAINES- This divorce petition was dismissed by the Ste. Genevieve Superior Court on March 13, 1815, when Mary failed to make a scheduled appearance.

Samuel STROTHER vs Mary STROTHER- Samuel failed to make a court appearance, so this petition, filed on March 13, 1815, in Ste. Genevieve Superior Court was dismissed.

Ruth BLACKBURN vs Benjamin BLACKBURN- This petition was filed by Ruth's father, Jacob JOHEVER, in 1816, in Ste. Genevieve Circuit Court. The Court ordered Ruth to return to her husband, and her father to pay costs.

Ferguson HAILE vs Jemima HAILE- On October 16, 1816, this petition was filed in Ste. Genevieve County Circuit Court. An alias summons was issued in St. Louis County on April 16, 1817, and the divorce was finalized on September 6, 1819.

Sally PETTIT, by her next friend Thomas PRIGHT vs John PETTIT-Filed on October 17, 1816, this divorce petition was later dismissed by the Ste. Genevieve Superior Court.

Mary MOORE, by her next friend, Samuel GILBERT vs Joseph MOORE- This divorce was granted by the Ste. Genevieve Superior Court on April 17, 1817.

Ezekiel ABLE vs Sarah ABLE- Filed in Cape Girardeau County on October 17, 1818, this petition was continued until April 22, 1819. On that date a witness, Robert CULLACH, failed to answer a subpoena. The divorce was granted on April 23, 1819.

Elizabeth BLAIR, by her next friend, Daniel DUNKLIN vs Silas BLAIR- This divorce petition was filed in 1818 in Washington County, and finalized on November 18, 1819.

Polly WEATHERS, by her next friend, John BRAVEN vs John WEATHERS- After this petition was filed on April 23, 1819 in Cape Girardeau County, the Court ruled there were insufficient grounds, and dismissed the suit.

Synthia TURDOTT, by her next friend, Henry BRYON vs Joseph TURDOTT- This petition, granted on July 10, 1819 by the St. Charles County Circuit Court, awarded Synthia three hundred dollars in back support, dating from June 1, 1817 when Joseph left. She was also to receive one hundred dollars per year after that.

Huldah DAVIS vs Harper C. DAVIS- Filed in Howard County, this divorce was granted on July 16, 1819.

Nancy EADS, by her next friend, John SIMPSON vs John EADS-Filed in the November term 1819, in Franklin County, this petition alleged John was guilty of illtreating Nancy and threatening to kill her before finally kicking her out. A jury found him guilty of three of the charges, but the petition was dismissed by the Court during the March term 1820.

Peggy (Margaret) BUTCHER vs Michael BUTCHER- This petition, filed on November 4, 1819 in Ste. Genevieve County, with a supplemental petition added on March 10, 1820. On June 12, 1821 Nancy DELEY of Perry County was called as a witness, but failed to appear. The petition was finalized on June 19, 1821.

William HILL vs Polly HILL- This divorce was granted on November 19, 1819 in Washington County.

Hugh McINTYRE vs Susanna McINTYRE- This petition, filed November 20, 1819 was dismissed by the Washington County Circuit Court during the November term 1820.

Mary DAVIS, by her next friend, Charles VALL vs Isaac DAVIS- Mary's attorney, Alexander BUCKNER, filed this petition on August 18, 1819, in Cape Girardeau County, and was granted on April 6, 1821.

Samuel SMILEY vs Daratha SMILEY- This petition was filed in St. Charles County on March 20, 1820, but after an order for publication was handed down by the Court, no other entries were recorded.

Jane PATTERSON vs James PATTERSON- Submitted in Cape Girardeau County on April 19, 1820, this petition for divorce was granted on August 15, 1821.

Elizabeth McCOY, by her next friend, John WOOD vs John McCOY- During a July 20, 1820, appearence in Howard County, Elizabeth stated she would not continue to seek a divorce.

Caleb MOORE vs Holday MOORE- Caleb's attorney, Johnson RANNEY, filed this Petition in Cape Girardeau County. On December 18, 1829. Holday appeared to deny the allegations. A jury consisting of John PIBEN, Christian GATES, John PIBEN, Jr., William SHEPPARD, Nicholas WHITLOW, William SURRELL, Andrew GIBONEY, John AIKEN, Thomas GRAVES, Thomas SULLINGER, Roland GREEN, and William FISHBACK found her innocent of the charges, and dismissed the petition.

Nancy EADS vs John EADS- This petition was filed during the January term 1821, in Gasconade County, but no other entries were made. Nancy had applied to the Franklin County Circuit Court for a divorce the year before.

Sarah LILLARD, by her next friend, David JENNINGS vs Jeremiah LILLARD- On the grounds Sarah feared for her life, this petition was filed on February 13, 1821, in Lafayette County, but later dropped on the advice of council.

John BAKER vs Nancy BAKER- This petition was filed in Washington County on March 20, 1821. On July 16, 1821, Nancy appeared to answer charges, and read an affidavit from John ANDREWS written in her behalf. The suit was dismissed.

Abraham JOHNSON vs Hannah JOHNSON- Filed during the March term 1821, in Franklin County, this petition was dropped after the Court handed down an order of publication.

Alexander TAYLOR vs Ann TAYLOR- After being filed on March 20, 1821, in Franklin County, no other entries were found for this case.

Adelaid RIGHT, by her next friend, Peter F. LAFORGE vs Jesse RIGHT- Filed on March 28, 1821, in New Madrid County, this divorce petition was later dropped.

Jane TAILOR, by her next friend, John LAND vs Archibald TAILOR-Charging willful absence and adultery, Jane filed for divorce on July 25, 1821, in New Madrid County. No other entries found.

Jane COOPER vs Braxton COOPER- Filed in Lillard (now Lafayette) County, this divorce petition alleged desertion as grounds. It was granted on October 10, 1821.

Samuel D. STROTHER vs Polly STROTHER- Samuel first filed for divorce in Ste. Genevieve County in 1815, but that petition was dropped when he failed to make a court appearance. Samuel filed the second time on April 29, 1822, in the Cape Girardeau County Circuit Court. He named his wife as Polly STROTHER, late Polly RODNEY. This petition was granted on August 16, 1822.

Ann TURNER vs Philip TURNER- Filed during the May term 1822, in Howard County, this petition was later dropped.

Joseph JACKSON vs Mary JACKSON- Joseph's attorney, Mr. HUNT, filed this divorce petition on the grounds of desertion, on April 14, 1823, in Pike County. The Court ordered depositions from witnesses in Oswego County, New York. The petition was denied during the August term 1824.

Katherine WINDES, by her next friend, Dubart MURPHY vs Samuel WINDES- This petition for divorce was filed on July 4, 1823, and granted on December 3, 1823, in St. Francois County. Katherine was awarded custody of their son, Franklin WINDES.

Sarah FOSTER vs Dabney FOSTER- This petition was filed on July 29, 1823, in Washington County, and continued through the next two terms of the court before being dropped.

Ludia HINSON vs Griffen HINSON, alias Nicholas OWENS- Filed during the July term 1823, in Clay County, this petition, was granted during the July term 1824.

Cornelius BURNET vs Jane BURNET- On August 2, 1823, this petition was filed in Washington County, but dropped on November 27th, at the request of the petitioner.

Nancy COTTLE, by her next friend, Samuel GILBERT vs Ira COTTLE- No grounds were stated in the Lincoln County Circuit Court Record on August 5, 1823, when this petition was filed. The petition was later dropped.

John WATSON vs Anna WATSON- John filed his petition for divorce by his attorney, Mr. EASTON, on August 15, 1823, in Pike County, on the grounds Anna had left him on September 15, 1821. An alias summons was issued for Mary WATSON, so the divorce was finalized in August of 1824.

Susan McDONALD, by her next friend, John SULLINS vs Benjamin McDONALD- This petition was filed on December 18, 1823, in Franklin County, and was granted on July 20, 1824.

William PATTON vs Martha PATTON- After he filed for divorce during the June term 1824, William was ordered to publish his petition in the *Missouri Intelligencer* for six weeks because Martha had left Boone County. William requested depositions be taken from witnesses in Davidson County, Tennessee.

Theodice BUTCHER, by her next friend, Charles GRIFFEN vs Benjamin BUTCHER- After filing her petition on July 14, 1824, in Ste. Genevieve County, Theodice was ordered to publish a notice of intent to seek a divorce. The divorce was granted March 15, 1825.

John DUNN vs Elizabeth DUNN- Filed on August 16, 1824, in Cape Girardeau, this petition was granted on December 17, 1824, but the verdict was set aside on December 21, 1824. On that date Elizabeth filed her own petition for divorce. Both suits were dropped.

Mary STRODE vs Stephen STRODE- In this petition, filed in Boone County, Mary requested custody of their children, and ownership of two slaves, Henry and Thomas, one horse, and six head of cattle. The divorce was granted on October 13, 1824.

Mary A. STIDGER, by her next friend, C.G. MOULS vs William R. STIDGER- This petition was filed during the October term 1824, in New Madrid County, where it was granted in the June term 1825.

Edward KELLY vs Mary KELLY- This petition was filed in the June term 1825, in Boone County on the grounds of adultery. The court found Mary had committed adultery, but had immediately confessed to her husband. Since Edward had continued to live with her for two years after the incident, his divorce petition was dismissed.

Jane HOPPER vs JOHN HOPPER- This divorce petition was filed on July 13, 1825 in Callaway County, but dismissed on July 10, 1826.

Malinda M'CARY vs Joseph M'CARY- Malinda filed for divorce in October of 1825, in New Madrid County, but dropped her petition on February 22, 1827, when John filed his own petition.

John DUNN vs Elizabeth DUNN- John had first filed for divorce in Cape Girardeau County. His second petition was filed in Washington County on January 5, 1826. In this petition, John stated he had married Elizabeth NEILE on July 6, 1820, and claimed she had left him on September 25, 1823. Once again Elizabeth filed her own petition. Both actions were dropped.

Ann GIBSON, by her next friend, John FRAZER vs William GIBSON- When Ann filed her petition on January 12, 1826, in Washington County, she asked for alimony and child support. She also presented affidavits from Pierre August LABEAUME and Walter WATSON concerning the case. The Court ordered William to pay five dollars per month in support.

Jeremiah LILLARD vs Sarah LILLARD- This petition, filed during the March term 1826, in Lafayette County, charged Sarah with adultery. On the same day the State of Missouri charged her with bigamy on an alias writ from Saline County.

Samuel SMILEY vs Elizabeth SMILEY- Samuel was first granted a divorce on October 3, 1826, in Lincoln County. An entry in the margin of the circuit court record has the notation, "This entry expunged. Entry will be found of Record Feby term 1827". On February 5, 1827, the court overturned the earlier ruling to include the finding that Samuel had not abused Elizabeth. The divorce was again granted on that date.

Last Will and Testament of Gresham FOREST- Entered into Callaway County Probate Court on June 13, 1826, this document held that, "My wife, previous to my removing from Kentucky made a settlement with me... and having preference to Mr. John WILLIAMS Esq., she relinquished all claims against me.".

Christian JOHNSON vs Peggy JOHNSON- This petition for divorce was filed on February 14, 1827, in New Madrid County. The petition was continued through three more terms before it was dropped.

Joseph M'CARY vs Malinda M'CARY- This petition was a counter-suit to one filed by Malinda in April of 1825. In his petition, Joseph claimed he was married in April of 1823 to Malinda SICCAY, and that she left him three weeks later. He also stated Malinda had lived with John WOODARD in a state of adultery for two years.
On June 5, 1827, The State of Missouri charged Joseph with bigamy. He was acquitted on February 9, 1828, and the divorce was finalized on June 5, 1828.

Joseph BAYER vs Sarah BAYER- On June 7, 1827, Sarah was charged with adultery by the State of Missouri. Soon after, Joseph filed for a divorce, and the petition was granted on October 5, 1827, in Gasconade County.

Milo FANNING vs Patzey FANNING- Filed in New Madrid County on February 8, 1828, this petition stated Milo married Patzey BARKER on July 9, 1822, at Jonesburg, Illinois. Milo claimed she had left him in June of 1826, for William HORO, and they had left the state. This petition was finalized on October 8, 1828.

Benjamin CARROLL vs Nancy CARROLL- This petition was filed on February 12, 1828, in Franklin County. On July 6, 1829, Benjamin appeared in Court and asked to have divorce action dropped.

William BROWN vs Barbara BROWN- This divorce petition was filed in Gasconade County on February 14, 1828, on the grounds that Barbara had committed adultery.

John CAMPELL vs Elizabeth CAMPELL- Citing desertion as the grounds, this petition was filed on February 14, 1828, in Gasconade County. No other action was taken.

Jane W. SIMPSON vs Vincent B. SIMPSON- In this petition Jane accused Vincent of leaving her destitute, and of living with another woman in Kentucky. When the petition was filed in St. Francois County on March 12, 1828, Jane asked for custody of the two children, Thompson and Matilda, which she got when the divorce was granted on July 15, 1828.

Abraham ZUMWALT vs Juliet ZUMWALT- Abraham and Juliet HOPE were married on September 26, 1825. In his petition for divorce, filed in Callaway County on March 13, 1828, Abraham stated that Juliet, "left...on October 5th, 1825, without just cause", when he filed on March 13, 1828. A divorce was granted on July 16, 1828.

Kinkead CALDWELL vs Mary CALDWELL- Filed during the April term 1828, in Franklin County, Kinkead claimed he and Mary were married on March 5, 1824, and she left him in 1826. This divorce was granted on June 11, 1828.

Peter GARBER vs Betsy GARBER- This petition was filed on April 12, 1828, in Pike County on the grounds Betsy had entered into a second marriage with John CONLEG. The divorce was finalized the same term.

Eleanor NOLAND vs Ashford NOLAND- After this petition was filed during the June term 1828 in Boone County, the Court ordered an alias writ issued in Jackson County.

Melisse BROWN, by her next friend, William McMURTREY vs Harbourt BROWN- Filed during the July term 1828, in Madison County, this divorce petition was not continued.

Lewis BARNES vs Polly BARNES- This divorce petition was filed during the October term 1828, in Boone County, and discontinued at the request of the petitioner.

Richard MORRISON vs Hepsebar MORRISON- After being filed in Cooper County Circuit Court in the October term 1828, this divorce petition was continued until February of 1831, when Richard told the court he no longer wished to sue for a divorce.

Sally DAUGHTERS vs Nicholas DAUGHTERS- On March 2, 1829, the Gasconade County Circuit Court ordered Sally to publish a notice of her proposed divorce action. If Nicholas did not appear by the first Thursday in July at the home of David WALDS, where court would be held, the petition would be granted.

Cealy CURTIS vs Enoch CURTIS- In March of 1829, the Chariton County Circuit Court ordered Cealy to publish her intention to sue for divorce. No further entries were made for this case.

Ann LAIRD vs David LAIRD- In her divorce petition, Ann claimed after she and David were married in July of 1820, David treating her in a cruel manner. He was accused of frequent and repeated drunkenness, and of beating her without provocation. When the petition was filed in Lincoln County on June 9, 1829, the Court waived the order of publication. Ann asked that her petition be dismissed on October 13, 1829.

Sarah HUBBARD, by her next friend, Abram B. KING vs Charles H. HUBBARD- This divorce petition was filed on June 9, 1829, in Lincoln County, and granted on October 13, 1829. Charles was ordered to pay fifty dollars in support on January 1, 1830, and to continue to pay that amount every year as long as Sarah stayed single.

Ardelia WOODBRIDGE, by her next friend, Martial COTTLE vs William W. WOODBRIDGE- After filing this petition on October 13, 1829, in Lincoln County, Ardelia was granted a divorce on February 9, 1830. At that time, William was ordered to pay her three hundred dollars, and one hundred dollars each year thereafter, if Ardelia remained single.

Nancy BELCHER vs Alexander BELCHER- This petition was filed in Boone County, and finalized during the October term 1829.

Catherine APPLEGATE, by her next friend, Amelia PEPPER vs Joseph APPLEGATE- When Catherine's solicitor, Mr. BENT, filed this petition in St. Francois Co. on Nov. 9, 1829, it claimed the two married in 1816, but four years prior to filing for divorce, Joseph had committed adultery. The petition was granted, March 1830.

Cynthia ORR, by her next friend, Thomas SUGGETT vs Jacob ORR- Filed on November 10, 1829, in Callaway County, this petition claims Joseph and Cynthia SWAN were married August 6, 1824, but that Jacob left on March 11, 1827. The divorce was granted on November 9, 1830.

Jacob STUART vs Lucinda STUART- This petition was filed in Callaway County during the November term 1829, but was later dropped.

Richard BESWELL vs Cynthia BESWELL- Filed July 3, 1830, in Madison County, this petition was dismissed by the Court during the February term 1831.

Agnes LAKEY, by her next friend, Garland HARDING vs Alexander LAKEY- After hearing the allegations made by both parties on July 6, 1830, the Franklin County Circuit Court ruled there were too many discrepancies in their stories. The case was dismissed on May 11, 1831.

Andrew CORN vs Lydia MASON, alias Lydia CORN- After Andrew and Lydia were married in July of 1829, in Cape Girardeau County, Alexander learned Lydia was still married to John MASEY. The divorce was granted immediately after a petition was submitted to the court on June 11, 1831.

Peter SAPP vs Patience SAPP- After this petition was filed in Boone County in 1832, no other action was taken.

Margaret FRANKLIN, by her next friend, David LEMON vs Thomas FRANKLIN- This divorce petition was filed in Crawford County on February 4, 1832, by Margaret's solicitor, John JAMISON Esq., and granted in August of 1833, on the grounds of desertion.

Aaron SPANN vs Anna SPANN- No further action was found concerning this petition after it was filed in Crawford County during the May term 1832.

Susan NICKLE vs James NICKLE- This petition for alimony was filed and granted on October 9, 1832, in Clay County.

William P. LITTLE vs Mary Ann LITTLE- In his petition for divorce, William stated he married May Ann YOUNG on March 15, 1831, in Randolph County, and on January 27, 1833, she married James EDISON (marriage records have January 16th) in Madison County. This divorce was granted in March of 1834.

Stephen GUERRANT vs Emily GUERRANT- Citing desertion as grounds, this petition was filed on December 18, 1832, in Callaway County, and finalized on October 11, 1833.

Jacob CARROLL vs Nancy CARROLL, formerly Nancy HILL- Jacob sued and was granted a divorce in 1834, in Gasconade County on the grounds of desertion.

Emily REMICK vs Samuel REMICK- This divorce petition was filed during the January term 1834, in Warren County. No further action was taken.

Enoch PENNY vs Ann PENNY- In this petition filed on February 25, 1834, in New Madrid County, Enoch stated he had married Ann HARRINGTON in 1821 (the rest of the entries for this year are illegible).

Margaret BRADLEY vs Benjamin BRADLEY- Filed in Monroe County in April of 1834, Margaret stated in her petition for alimony and divorce she would drop her petition if Benjamin would voluntarily return home. If not, she asked the court to order him to take his suit of clothes, and leave immediately. No further action found.

Susanna WESTOVER vs George WESTOVER- This petition for divorce, filed on March 7, 1834, in St. Francois County, charged George with extreme cruelty. It was finalized in the March term 1835.

John S. MORELAND vs Ann MORELAND- In his petition, filed during the June term 1834, in Cooper County, John claimed Ann had been gone more than two years. The divorce was granted in October of 1834.

John ROCKHOLD vs Jane ROCKHOLD- This petition was filed in Ray County in June of 1834, on the grounds that Jane had committed adultery with William GREEN. John was granted a divorce on October 13, 1834.

Henry HOWARD vs Rebeckah HOWARD- In his petition, filed in Ralls County on January 14, 1835, Henry stated he married Rebeckah ALFREY on March 1, 1828. After Rebeckah was ordered to appear on the first Monday in June of the following year, no other entries were made for this case.

Mary HODGES vs Peter B. HODGES- After this petition was filed in Cole County during the February term 1835, Peter was ordered to appear on March 5, 1835, to answer charges. On September 22, 1835, Mary asked the Court to dismiss her petition.

Henry PROBST, by his attorney, Abel WATLENS vs Sarah PROBST- After hearing this petition, which was filed in Cape Girardeau County on February 4, 1835, the Court ordered a summons issued for Sarah in Madison County. No other entries were made for this divorce action.

Joseph KETCHUM vs Sarah KETCHUM- This divorce was granted on February 19, 1835, in Clay County.

James CARSON vs Susannah CARSON- When James filed this divorce petition in Ralls County during the February term 1835, he asked the Court to grant him Sarah's inheritance from her father, James LEADFORD. He was granted a divorce during the July term 1835, on the grounds of desertion.

Joab MOBERLEY vs Sally MOBERLEY- After Joab filed for divorce in April of 1835, in Ralls County, Sally was ordered to appear and answer charges on the first Monday of the July term. In August of 1836, the Court ruled it did not have jurisdiction over this case.

Agnes REYNOLDS, by her next friend, George CRAIG vs Thomas REYNOLDS- Agnes appeared during the April term 1835, and produced an affidavit from Weston F. BIRCH of Howard County, that notice of her divorce petition had been published in the *Western Monitor*. This divorce was granted on August 15, 1836, and Agnes was awarded eighty dollars per year, dating from June of 1831, for her support.

Dolly MILLER, by her next friend, French GLASCOCK vs Allison E. MILLER- This petition was filed in Ralls County on June 9, 1835. Dolly claimed that from June 1831 to December 25, 1834 when he left, Allison was guilty of cruel and inhumane treatment, and that until July 15, 1835, he had continued an adulterous relationship with a slave named Maria. Dolly also petitioned the Court for custody of their daughter, Dolly. This petition was denied by the Court.

Elizabeth BEST vs Humphrey BEST- In her petition for divorce, filed in Clay County on July 21, 1835, Elizabeth also asked for alimony. On that day an alias writ was issued for Humphrey in Carroll County. On May 13, 1836, Elizabeth petitioned the Court to prevent Joel TURNHAM and John C. HAWKINS from turning over the money they had been holding for Humphrey. Humphrey filed suit on March 22, 1837, but the next day TURNHAM and HAWKINS were ordered to give the money to Elizabeth.

Walds LITTLEFIELD vs Mercy LITTLEFIELD- On the grounds of adultery and desertion, Walds filed for divorce on July 22, 1835, in Clay County. The petition was dismissed on March 21, 1836.

Tabathy YORK vs James YORK- This petition was filed in Howard County on July 27, 1835. After an appearance in March of 1836, no other entries were recorded for this divorce action.

Mahaleth MILLER vs James MILLER- Filed on February 13, 1836, in Howard County, this divorce petition was dropped in July at the request of the petitioner. In November of 1838, James filed suit against Mahaleth, but this petition was dismissed by the Court.

John WITT vs Elizabeth WITT- In his divorce petition which was filed in August of 1836, in Monroe County, John claimed Elizabeth had borne another man's child. Elizabeth counter-charged on the grounds that John was habitually intoxicated and that he beat her. The court ordered both petitions dismissed.

Henry PALMER vs Lydia Ann PALMER- This petition was dismissed by the Monroe County Circuit Court in August 1836.

Susan GENTRY vs David GENTRY- After this divorce petition was filed in August of 1836, in Monroe County, Susan was given custody of the children, and all the property on December 6, 1836.

Maressa FOLEY vs Adam CORNELIUS- Maressa, represented by Peyton R. HAYDEN, presented an affidavit of proof that her petition for annulment had been published. The Morgan County Circuit Court declared the marriage null and void in September of 1836, but later decided it did not have jurisdiction, because the order for publication was from another county.

Lydia Ann PALMER vs Henry PALMER- After this petition was filed in Monroe County during the March term 1837, Henry filed a motion to have Lydia's petition set aside. No further action was recorded.

Mary HAGEN vs David HAGEN- David answered a summons issued in this divorce action on July 19, 1837, in Clay County. Nothing else was recorded after that date.

Sophia GATSON vs Smith GATSON- This petition was filed on July 21, 1837, by Sophia's solicitor, Philip WILLIAMS, in Monroe County, but dismissed at the request of the petitioner on November 21, 1837.

Jacentha FOURTER vs Thomas FOURTER- No further action was taken on this divorce petition after it was filed in Clinton County during the November term 1837.

Permelia MORRIS vs Daniel MORRIS- On November 20, 1837, Permelia filed for support in Monroe County Circuit Court.

Pamelia LIPSCOMB vs Wade LIPSCOMB- This petition was filed during the December term 1837, and continued in Greene County.

Larkin DUMAS vs Eliza DUMAS- In this petition, filed in New Madrid County, Larkin stated he and Elizabeth HARRINGTON were married in 1832. The divorce was granted on July 14, 1838, on the grounds of adultery.

William HOPE vs Elizabeth HOPE- Filed on July 14, 1838, in New Madrid County, this divorce petition was continued through each term until the last entry in the March term 1839.

William C. SMITH vs Elizabeth SMITH- After this divorce petition was filed in Clinton County in the July term 1838, no other entries were made.

John JACKSON vs Eleanor JACKSON- This petition was filed in 1839, in Gasconade County. John told the Court he and Eleanor were married on February 18, 1836, in Illinois, but that she had left him. John was ordered to publish his divorce petition, and if Eleanor did not appear in Court to answer the complaint, the divorce would be granted.

Ann GUM vs John GUM- Ann filed her petition in Platte County during the March term 1839. John was also indicted for gambling during the same term. On July 22, 1839, witnesses testified that John was a habitual drunkard. After listening to the witnesses, the Court granted this petition on that day.

Josephine J.WINTER vs Samuel P.WINTER- Charging her husband with extreme cruelty, and of being a habitual drunkard, Josephine filed her petition in Platte County on July 23, 1839. If Samuel did not respond to the charges before the November term, it would be taken as an admission of guilt, and the divorce would be granted.

Margaret HUMPHREY vs David HUMPHREY- This divorce petition was filed on July 31, 1839, in Greene County, but later dismissed.

Charles BUTLER vs Margaret BUTLER- When this petition was filed during the August term 1839, in Macon County. An order of publication was given, and if Margaret did not respond, the divorce would be granted during the June term 1840.

Mary KAHILL vs Thomas KAHILL- Filed during the August term 1839, in Polk County, this petition for divorce was granted during the August term 1840.

Elizabeth P. LIPSCOMB vs Wade LIPSCOMB- After Wade had successfully stopped Elizabeth from getting a divorce in Greene County in 1837, she filed this petition during the April term in Polk County. In this petition, Elizabeth again asked for custody of their daughter, Lucy Ann, plus custody of an infant, Margaret. This petition was also denied.

Benjamin ROUNCE vs Mrs. C. ROUNCE- This petition for divorce was filed and dismissed during the May term 1839, in Chariton County.

Heller JONES vs Louisa JONES- Henry filed a petition for divorce on November 16, 1839, in New Madrid County on the grounds that when he married Louisa in 1837, she was still the wife of John POOL, whom she married in 1834. This petition was granted on March 13, 1840.

Catherine FOWLER, by her next friend, Charles P. BULLOCK vs William FOWLER- After this petition was filed in Henry County in the November term, the court ordered the plaintiff to dismiss her divorce action during the March term 1840.

Sarah E. LINN vs William LINN- In this petition for an annulment, filed in Benton County during the December term 1839, Sarah requested she be awarded custody of their son (not named). No other entries were recorded for this case.

Frances REDMAN vs Francis REDMAN- This petition filed in Benton County during the December term 1839, claims Francis willfully deserted and absented himself. If he did not appear and answer the charges by August 17, 1840, the petition would be granted.

David LAKE vs Mary LAKE- No other entries were recorded for this divorce action after it was filed in Benton County on December 22, 1839.

Mary PORTERFIELD vs John N. PORTERFIELD- This divorce petition was filed and granted in Gasconade County in 1839.

Henry ROOF vs Michal ROOF- After this petition was filed during the December term 1839, it went to trial. In April of 1840, a jury found the case to be a true bill, but was later dismissed by the court.

Lucinda ANDERSON vs James ANDERSON- Lucinda claimed James had been gone for more than two years when she filed for divorce in Miller County in 1839. Only one entry was found for this petition.

James YOUNG vs Polly YOUNG- On March 27, 1840, James appeared in Platte County Circuit Court, and proved his allegations were true. This divorce petition was granted on July 31, 1840.

Miles M. SEE vs Mary Ann SEE- A summons was returned to the Livingston County Circuit Court on April 24, 1840, showing that Mary could not be found in that county. This divorce petition was dismissed at the request of the plaintiff in December of 1840.

Nathaniel WICE vs Rhoda WICE- This petition was ordered continued after being filed in Platte County on July 27, 1840. No other entries were made in the court record.

Elvira WELLS vs Joshua SMITH- This case was filed for a breach of marriage contract in Ray County. The trial was held during the August term 1840, and the jury awarded Elvira forty-five dollars and eighty-seven cents in damages.

Rhess M. VANDERFORD vs Mary VANDERFORD- Rhess charged Mary with cruel treatment and desertion when he filed this divorce petition in Polk County in August of 1840. The petition was dismissed by the Court during the March term 1841.

Thomas DAVIDSON vs Isabella DAVIDSON- In this petition filed in the August term 1840, in Polk County, Thomas stated Isabella had left numerous times before, but always came back. This time she had been gone more than two years. This divorce was granted in the July term 1841.

Jane MORRIS vs Beauford S. MORRIS- This petition was granted in Daviess County after Beauford failed to make a court appearance at the August term 1840.

Urban E. CHISHAM vs America CHISHAM- In this petition filed in Lewis County during the November term 1840, Parker TATE was named as a witness, and America confessed to the charges leveled against her. This divorced was granted the following year.

John WEIR vs Mary WEIR- After this petition was filed in Gasconade County in 1841, John told the Court he would not continue to prosecute this case.

Nancy SMATHERS vs John SMATHERS- Nancy filed this petition for divorce in Miller County on March 30, 1841. She claimed they were married in October of 1838, and the following July, John left her without just cause. This divorce was granted on April 4, 1842.

John CHANEY vs Elizabeth CHANEY- After being filed during the April term 1841, in Livingston County, this petition for divorce was dropped.

James COOK vs Mary COOK- Mary answered the summons for her husband's petition against her during the April term 1841, at the Livingston County Circuit Court. After that this petition was dropped.

William SLATTER vs Elizabeth SLATTER- During the June term 1841, the Ray County Circuit Court ordered Elizabeth to appear during the next term. No other entries were made in regard to this case.

Amanda LEGANS vs Daniel LEGANS- Citing desertion as grounds for the divorce, Amanda filed her petition in Jasper County in July of 1841. She claimed that she and Daniel were married in February of 1837, and that Daniel left on March 10, 1839. The divorce was granted in October of 1841.

Elijah S. ROOK vs Nancy ROOK- After filing for divorce in July of 1841, Elijah asked for a delay during the same term. He returned to the Polk County Circuit Court in November of 1842, and requested the petition be dismissed.

Emaline DODD vs Benjamin DODD- This divorce petition was filed in Macon County in August of 1841, and when it was granted during the December term of the same year, Benjamin was ordered to pay five hundred dollars in alimony.

Mary DAVIS vs John DAVIS- When Mary filed her petition for divorce in Miller County on August 5, 1841, she stated she and John were married in 1825. Mary accused him of committing adultery in 1840, after which, they separated. This petition was granted on April 4, 1842.

Sarah AUBIN vs Peter AUBIN- Sarah told the Court she and Peter were married in 1837, and after that he left. Petition granted on November 19, 1841, in New Madrid County.

James H. CASH vs Elizabeth CASH- This petition was filed in Platte County on November 23, 1841, and continued through a number of terms before being discontinued in 1843.

Nancy PORE vs Thomas PORE- No other entries were found for this divorce, which was petitioned on November 24, 1841, in Platte County.

Isaac GIBSON vs Mary GIBSON- This petition was filed after the State brought charges against Mary for bigamy in Cass County in 1842. Mary's other husband was named as William M. MARSHALL, and Mary plead guilty during the July term 1843. Isaac was granted a divorce during the same term. Mary was sentenced to four days imprisonment, and fined twenty dollars by the Court.

Mary HUNT vs Abraham HUNT- After the Henry County Court ordered Mary to publish a notice of her intention to sue for divorce during March of 1842, this petition was dropped.

Elizabeth DALEY vs John DALEY- In March of 1842, the Daviess County Circuit Court ruled that if John did not appear to answer the charges leveled against him in this petition, a divorce would be granted in the September term.

Mattie BUGLEOH vs Susan BUGLEOH- This petition was filed on March 24, 1842, in New Madrid County. On September 25, 1843, Mattie stated he had married Susan BOOKER on October 7, 1837. A divorce was granted on March 28, 1844.

Mary NORMAN vs Aquilla NORMAN- After they were married in December of 1840, Mary learned Peter had a wife still living. This petition was granted on March 26, 1842 in New Madrid County.

Henrietta SWARTZ vs Henry SWARTZ- On the grounds of desertion, this petition was heard by Judge Priestley H. McBRIDE on March 29,

1842. Proof that the divorce petition had been published was submitted to the Court on July 26, 1842, but there were no entries made in the Scotland County records after that date.

Sanford DARNALL vs Sarah DARNALL- After being filed in Scotland County on March 30, 1842, this petition was later dismissed at the request of the plaintiff.

James HEREFORD vs Elizabeth HEREFORD- This petition was submitted by James' solicitor, James R. ABERNATHY, on March 30, 1842, in Scotland County. No other entries were recorded.

George W. SMITH vs Orlina SMITH- After George filed for a divorce in March of 1842 in Jasper County, he amended the petition during the same term to include that he and Orlina were married in May of 1838, but Orlina left him the next February. This divorce was granted during the July term 1842.

Allen SCOTT vs Jane SCOTT- No further action was taken on this petition after it was filed in Grundy Co. during the April term 1842.

Charles F. GIBBS vs Elizabeth GIBBS- This divorce petition was filed in April of 1842 in Linn County, and was granted on August 19, 1842.

Jacob VANDUZEN vs Polly VANDUZEN- After this divorce petition was filed in Chariton County in March of 1842, alias writs were issued in both Chariton and Macon County. Jacob dropped his petition during the March term 1843.

Mary Jane HOLIDAY vs John D. HOLIDAY- John was ordered to appear during the December term after this divorce petition was filed in Pettis County on May 23, 1842. The petition was granted in the July term 1843, and Mary was awarded custody of their daughter, Elizabeth.

Matilda WHEELER vs Oliver WHEELER- In the July term 1842, permission was given to the plaintiff to file an amended bill for divorce in Crawford County.

Archibald M. SMITH vs Caroline C. SMITH- This petition claimed that soon after the couple was married on August 7, 1839, Caroline left. Filed on July 1, 1842, this petition was granted on April 26, 1843, in Jasper County.

Martha MAKINSON vs Evan MAKINSON- This petition was granted in Linn County on August 20, 1842 by a jury which awarded Martha five hundred dollars in alimony.

Sharps H. TAYLOR vs Nancy TAYLOR- Filed in Macon County in August of 1842, this petition was granted during the May term 1844.

Benjamin F. STEPHENS vs Sally STEPHENS- After this petition was filed in Chariton County on October 5, 1842, it was dismissed by the Court.

David WILSON vs Sarah Ann WILSON- In his petition filed in Scotland County on October 26, 1842, David claimed he and Sarah were married in Ohio in 1837, and they settled in William County, Ohio. During that time Sarah committed adultery. This bill for divorce was dismissed in December of 1843.

Wilkenson FLETCHER vs Nancy FLETCHER- After this petition for divorce was filed in Jasper County on October 29, 1842, Wilkenson asked the Court to dismiss it. Wilkenson was ordered to pay Nancy's court costs in 1844.

Orlena McDONALD vs Wm. H. McDONALD- This petition was filed in Miller County on December 6, 1842, and a divorce was granted in December of 1843.

Zachariah WELLS vs Polly WELLS- In this petition, filed in Grundy County during the April term 1843, Polly was given custody of their youngest child for five years, for which she would be given thirty dollars for support. Then Zachariah was to have the child. Filed on the grounds of adultery, this petition was granted in October of 1843.

William P. BRADEN vs Nancy BRADEN- William filed his in the next term. The Holt County Circuit Court dismissed his petition on March 2, 1844, and Nancy's in August of 1844.

Easterann PACKWOOD vs Larkin PACKWOOD- This petition was filed by Easterann's attorney, John W. KALLEY, in May of 1843. When it was dropped in the same term, the court ordered Larkin to pay the court costs.

Warren McDANIEL vs Rebecca McDANIEL- In this petition filed in May of 1843, Warren told the court he and Rebecca were married in

December of 1830. The Carroll County Circuit Court granted this divorce during the September term 1843.

Emily MORGAN vs John MORGAN- This petition was filed in Carroll County in the May term 1843, with the couple's marriage date given as October 14, 1835, by Emily. John had been gone more than two years when the petition was filed. Granted by the Court during the September term 1843.

Nancy KIRKPATRICK vs John KIRKPATRICK- Nancy and John were married on January 24, 1839, and he left in 1841, according to this petition filed during the May term 1843 in Carroll County. A divorce was granted in March of 1844.

Mary TOUT vs Charles TOUT- After proof of publication of the divorce petition was submitted to the Macon County Circuit Court in May of 1843, a divorce was granted during the November term 1843.

Abner GILSTRAP vs Peggy GILSTRAP- The sheriff of Macon County testified in May of 1843 that he had served papers on Peggy. The divorce was granted during the May term 1844.

Allen SCOTT vs Jane SCOTT- This petition was filed in June of 1843, and granted in April of 1844, in Daviess County. Allen had also filed for divorce in Grundy County in 1842.

John TINKLE vs Franny TINKLE- When he filed for divorce in June of 1843 in Andrew County, John claimed he and Franny were married in November of 1830. After that Franny became very abusive, to the point where John considered his life unbearable. This petition was dismissed during the March term 1844.

Nancy BURROWS vs Arthur BURROWS- There were no other entries for this divorce petition after it was filed in Holt County during the June term 1843.

Sarah DUNCAN vs James DUNCAN- After this petition was filed during the June term, an alias writ was issued in Clay County. A jury was convened to hear the case on March 5, 1845, but Sarah asked that her petition be dismissed by the Andrew County Circuit Court.

John HARTMAN vs Eliza HARTMAN- This petition for divorce was filed in Andrew County in June of 1843. John claimed he and Eliza were married in January of 1839, and that she had been gone more than two years when he filed. When John did not appear in Court on September 15, 1845, the petition was dismissed.

Susan WINCHESTER vs James WINCHESTER- When this petition was filed in New Madrid County on September 25, 1843, Susan stated she and John were married on May 25, 1835, in Tennessee, and he deserted her on March 15, 1841, after they moved to Missouri. This petition was granted on March 29, 1844.

Louise CADIEN vs Alexander CADIEN- Filed in New Madrid County on September 29, 1843, this petition claimed the couple was married in November of 1832. Alexander was charged with leaving in June of 1837. No further action was recorded for this divorce suit.

Robert WHITE vs Roccinda WHITE- This petition was filed in Daviess County during the October term 1843, and granted in October of 1844.

Washington KEESTER vs Ann Eliza KEESTER- Filed in Grundy County in October of 1843, Washington charged Ann with adultery. During the same term, Ann filed a motion for security against him, when he refused during the following April term, this divorce petition was dismissed by the Court.

John CASE vs Sarah CASE- After this petition was filed in Livingston County during the October term 1843, John filed a motion to suppress the deposition given by Adaline BRIN in June of 1845, which was denied. The court also denied a request for reimbursement for Sarah's room and board submitted by John GRAVES. This divorce was granted in the April term 1846.

Ann REDDING vs Joseph REDDING- This petition was filed in Daviess County during the October term 1843, and granted in the October term 1844.

E. VISTAL vs N. VISTAL- After filing his petition for divorce during the November term 1843, in Daviess County, E. VISTAL told the Court he would not continue to prosecute.

Glenn OWEN vs Catherine OWEN- This petition, filed in Pettis County in December of 1843, claimed Glenn married Catherine on June 10, 1841, and she left him on September 13th of the same year. A divorce was granted during the April term 1844.

Eliza RAYBURN vs William RAYBURN- This petition was filed in April of 1843, and dismissed by a jury in Grundy County in 1844.

Harriett McVAY vs Thomas McVAY- After this petition was filed in May of 1844, Thomas was ordered to appear at the November term. No other entries were made for this case in Daviess County.

Mary M. CASNER vs Eblen CASNER- When Mary filed her petition for divorce in Carroll County during the March term 1844, she told the Court that her children were adults. This petition was granted in the March term of 1845.

Eve Levina KEENER vs Martin KEENER- Filed on March 29, 1844, in New Madrid County, Eva claimed she had been deserted. No other entries were made after that date.

Polly Ann JENNINGS vs William C. JENNINGS- Polly claimed she and William were married December 1, 1840, and he left her on March 10, 1841. She filed for divorce during the April term 1844, in Pettis County. The divorce was granted in October of 1844.

Caroline ST. CLAIR vs Charles G. ST. CLAIR- In April of 1844, Charles failed to make a Court ordered appearence in Livingston County. No further entries were made for this case.

Ann EDMUNDSON vs Isaac EDMUNDSON- This petition, filed in Cass County in April of 1844, was later dismissed by the Court.

Elizabeth THOMAS vs J.L. THOMAS- This petition was filed in Macon County in May of 1844, and dismissed in 1845.

Mary A. HOLDERMAN vs Michael W. HORINE- Mary sued for breach of promise of marriage on May 30, 1844, in Jefferson County Circuit Court. She later testified she and Michael had settled the matter, and she dropped the suit.

Ellizabeth THOMAS vs J.L. THOMAS- Filed May 8, 1844, in Macon County on the grounds of desertion, this divorce petition was dropped after an order of publication was made.

Nancy BRADEN vs William P. BRADEN- This divorce petition was filed in Andrew County in the September term 1844, and granted on March 5, 1845. Both Nancy and William had sued for divorce in Holt County in 1843, but both of those petitions were dismissed by the Court.

Patrick M. DARCY vs Dicey DARCY- This petition was filed in Carroll County in September of 1844 (rest of record is missing).

Ann KEISTER vs Washington KEISTER- Ann presented proof of publication of her divorce petition during the September term 1844. A divorce was granted in May of 1845. Washington had sued Ann for divorce in Grundy County in 1843, but that petition was dismissed.

Susannah MILLER vs Samuel MILLER-This petition was filed in Andrew County in September of 1844, on the grounds of cruelty. Susannah told the Court she and Samuel were married on March 6, 1842. The Court ruled that if Samuel did not appear to answer the charges on March 3, 1846, a divorce would be granted.

Eiliza REYNOLDS vs James REYNOLDS- The Cass County Circuit Court dismissed this petition during the October term 1844, when neither party appeared.

Artimissia DANNON vs George DANNON- This petition was filed on October 31, 1844, and dismissed on May 2, 1845, in Jasper County.

Frederick ARRENT vs Sarah ARRENT- This petition was filed in Andrew County in the March term 1845, but dropped when Frederick failed to appear. Frederick later sent a divorce petition from Chariton County to the Missouri Legislature.

Joan PARKER vs Tomas F. PARKER- After this petition was filed in Andrew County during the March term 1845, the court ordered Thomas to appear at the March term 1846, or the divorce would be granted.

Mary Jane HOGAN vs Tilford HOGAN- In April of 1845, the Daviess County Circuit Court ruled that if Tilford did not appear at the next term, the divorce would be final.

Hardin CORNSTOCK vs Analiga CORNSTOCK- This petition was filed in April of 1845, and continued to 1846, in Livingston County.

Del___ F. FORBES vs Phebe E. FORBIS- This petition for divorce was filed in May of 1845, and granted on April 30, 1846 in Jasper County.

Joseph HURST vs Rhoda HURST- When he filed his petition in Andrew County during the September term 1845, Joseph told the

Court Rhoda was living in Buchanan County, and asked that a summons be issued in that county.

Amanda POWELL vs William K. POWELL- After this petition was filed during the September term 1845, in New Madrid County, it was continued to 1846.

Christianna GOETZ vs John GOETZ- This petition was filed in Gasconade County in September of 1845, and continued.

Rocilla ROGUS vs William ROGUS- This petition for divorce was granted in September of 1845, and Rocilla was awarded custody of their child in Livingston County.

Mary PHILLEBAR vs Peter PHILLEBAR- This petition was filed in New Madrid County on the grounds of cruel treatment and desertion. On September 24, 1845, proof of publication of the divorce petition was presented to the Court, and the petition was continued.

Patterson C. BRUMLEY vs Lucinda BRUMLEY- Filed in Miller County in October of 1845, this petition was continued through 1846.

Caroline RUTLAIGE vs William RUTLEDGE- This petition for divorce was finally granted in the September term 1845, in Livingston County.

Merton BRASFIELD vs Jane BRASFIELD- On October 31, 1845, Merton presented his deposition to the Court that he and Jane were married in February 1834, and at the time the divorce petition was filed, Jane had been gone more than two years. The divorce was granted on April 29, 1846, in Jasper County.

James WYRICK vs Mary WYRICK- Filed in Miller County during the October term 1845, this divorce petition was continued through 1846.

Vol. 1, No. 4, Aug 12, 1808. NOTICE- I will pay no debts of her (Sarah) contracting...John MENUS, July 27, 1808.

Vol. 1, No. 6, Aug 17, 1808. NOTICE- Whereas my wife Polly has left my bed and board, I will pay no debts of her contracting. Thomas BEAVERS, August 8, 1808.

Vol. 1, No. 6, Aug 24, 1808. William MONTGOMERY vs Nancy MONTGOMERY- Married on January 19, 1800, the couple lived together until January 20, 1805. Nancy was charged with committing adultery in Kentucky where she was believed to have gone. Also included was a deposition from Moses AUSTIN, stating William came to Missouri in 1798. Nancy was ordered to appear on the first Monday of the May term 1819, in St. Louis.

Vol. 1, No. 15, Nov 2, 1808. NOTICE- Whereas my wife Mary left my bed and board on Sunday, October 23rd, I forbid any person from advancing her anything in my name. Alexander BELLESIME, St. Louis, Oct 26, 1808.

Vol. 1, No. 30, July 5, 1809. NOTICE- I forewarn any person from harbouring or crediting her (Sarah) on my account. Walter DEWITT, June 25, 1809.

Vol. 3, No. 106, Aug 2, 1810. Jane PATTERSON, by her next friend, Benjamin MEYERS vs Eleazor PATTERSON- This petition, filed on the grounds of desertion, noted the couple were married in March of 1805. Eleazor was charged with leaving on February 20, 1806. He was ordered to appear at the May term 1811, in Ste. Genevieve District Court.

Vol. 3, No. 108, Aug 16, 1810. Pelagie ROBIN, by her next friend, Jean Baptiste VALLE vs Charles ROBIN- Pelagie and Charles were married on February 5, 1799 according to the petition. Charles was accused of deserting her on August 20, 1805. This petition was filed March 1, 1810 in St. Louis, and Charles was ordered to appear on the first Monday of the October term 1810.

Rebekah PAGET, by her next friend, John BAKER vs Henry PAGET- This petition, filed in Ste. Genevieve County, alleges that after Rebekah and Henry were married on March 12, 1797, Henry committed adultery on a regular basis, and he finally deserted her and the children. He was ordered to appear on the first Monday of the October term 1811, in St. Louis.

Rebekah HUNTER, by her next friend, Henry DODGE, and her attorney, Andrew SCOTT vs James HUNTER- This petition, filed March 17, 1810, claimed Rebekah and Andrew were married January 4, 1804. James was charged with deserting Rebekah and the family after beating and wounding his wife. He was ordered to appear on the first Monday of the May term 1811.

Vol. 3, No. 119, Oct 31, 1810. NOTICE- I will pay no contracts of Rosanna L. NASH to whom I was once married. Ira NASH, October 22, 1810.

Vol. 3, No. 148, May 23, 1811. NOTICE- Rebecca, my wife, has this day eloped from my bed and board in the district of St. Louis and township of Joachim. James ANDERSON, May 14, 1811.

Vol. 4, No. 138, Aug 1, 1811. NOTICE- Whereas my wife Mary has left my bed and board without reasonable cause....J. GLASS, July 3, 1811.

NOTICE- I will pay no debts of her contracting (Ruth) after this date...Isaac WEST, Goshen, July 24, 1811.

Vol. 4, No. 161. Aug 22, 1811. NOTICE- I will pay no debts of her (Lucinda) contracting...John BROWNSON, Fort Osage.

Vol. 5, No. 254, July 3, 1813. NOTICE- The public are hereby cautioned against trusting of in any manner bargaining with my wife Margarette, formerly Margarette LEPONSE...Benjamin DUBAI, St. Louis, July 1, 1813.

Vol. 5, No. 260, Aug 21, 1813. Margaret JONES vs William JONES- On March 15, 1813, the Hon. Wm. SPRIGGS, Esq., ordered the publication of this petition. William ordered to appear on the first Monday of May 1814, in Ste. Genevieve County, or in St. Louis on the first Monday in October of 1814.

Vol. 6, No. 279, Dec 25, 1813. NOTICE- ...caution the public from crediting my wife Celest in any manner as she refuses to co-habitate with me. Joseph LONGEVENT.

Vol. 6, No. 275, Jan 8, 1814. NOTICE- The public are hereby warned from crediting any one of my family as I will not pay any debts... Alexandre BELLESIME, January 8, 1814.

Vol. 6, No. 276, Jan 15, 1814. NOTICE- ...cautioned against crediting my wife Lenore, formerly Lenore MENARD who left my bed and board without just cause. Joseph HORITZ, January 2, 1814.

Vol. 6, No. 294, May 21, 1814. NOTICE- Whereas my wife Catherine having left my bed and board and having conducted herself in an adulterous manner... Samuel PRUETT.

Vol. 6, No. 300, July 2, 1814. NOTICE- Is hereby given by the subscriber that I will pay no debts which my wife, formerly Prouix CHANCELLIER, may contract. Basil PROUIX, St.Charles, July 1, 1814.

Vol. 6, No. 307, Aug 20, 1814. NOTICE- Whereas my wife, Anna has left my bed and board without just cause or provocation... Thomas WELCH, St. Louis, August 17, 1814.

Vol. 7, No. 313, October 1, 1814. NOTICE- Whereas my wife, Elizabeth, who contrary to her duty, has left my bed and board... Aaron TODD, Joachime Twp., St. Louis, September 30, 1814.

Vol. 7, No. 324, Dec 17, 1814. A CAUTION- I do forewarn any person from harboring her (Elizabeth) or dealing with her on my account... Paul WHILTEY, St. Louis Co., December 13, 1814.

Vol. 7, No. 343, June 3, 1815. NOTICE- I do hereby caution all parties from harboring her (Mary)...Jean Baptiste CREELY.

Vol. 7, No. 350, June 17, 1815. NOTICE- Nancy CESNER having left my bed and board and having sworn a false oath against me of being afraid for her life at my hands even though she slept with me the night before she took this wicked oath...Solomon CESNER, Florissant June 13, 1815.

Vol. 7, No. 360, Aug 26, 1815. NOTICE- ...against bargaining with or crediting on my account, my wife, Genevieve, formerly Genevieve RICHARD, who has deserted from me. Baptiste MOUSETTE, Aug 19.

Vol. 8, No. 393, April 6, 1816. NOTICE- Particularly to Tavern Keepers and Store Keepers- I will not pay any of her (Mary Josette ROY) contracting from this date. Ante. RANCONTRE, April 5, 1816.

Vol. 8, No. 396, Apr 27, 1816. NOTICE- Whereas my wife Mary, contrary to her duty has left...Angis GILLIS, St. Chas. Co., April 15, 1816.

Vol. 8, No. 402, June 15, 1816. NOTICE- ...as she (Mary) has threatened to fell my property, I hereby notify all persons not to buy or receive bills of sale as I will protect my property. Joel LASSITER, St. Louis Co., June 14, 1816.

Vol. 8, No. 408, July 27, 1816. Francois DEROIN charged his wife with deserting him.

Vol. 8, No. 410, Aug 10, 1816. NOTICE- Whereas my wife Cynthia has left my bed and board, I will pay no debts of her contracting. Anthony THOMAS, August 8, 1816.

Vol. 9, No. 417, Sept 28, 1816. NOTICE- I am determined not to pay any debts of her (Sally) contracting...William CRAWFORD.

Vol. 9, No. 431, Jan 4, 1817. NOTICE-...warned from contracting any debts with the said Mary MOREAUX COLLENS...L.S. COLLENS, Florisant, January 1, 1817.

Vol. 9, No. 432, Jan, 11, 1817. NOTICE- Whereas my wife Nancy EDDS has left my bed and board and acted in a very unbecoming manner...John EDDS, Burge Creek, Missouri Territory, January 1, 1817.

Vol. 9, No. 433, Jan 18, 1817. Felicite (VALLE) REGNIER, by her next friend, John J. COUJON vs Francois REGNIER- Grounds not stated. Francois ordered to appear on the second Monday of the April term 1817, at Jackson, Cape Girardeau County.

Vol. 9, No. 411, Mar 15, 1817. NOTICE- I will pay none of her (Catherine) debts or contracts after this date. Domenico HORTIS, St. Louis, March 13, 1817.

Vol. 9, No. 421, May 24, 1817. NOTICE- The public are hereby cautioned against crediting my wife, formerly Victoire MORIN, as she behaved herself imprudently...Peter DEBBIN, March 20, 1917.

Vol. 10, No. 479, Dec 6, 1817. NOTICE- The public are hereby notified not to make any contracts with my wife, Doratha who has left...Samuel SMILEY, St. Charles, December 3, 1817.

Vol. 10, No. 497, April 10, 1818. Sally WICKS, by her next friend, John S. BRICKEY, vs William WICKS- Married in July of 1811, Sally and William lived together until January of 1815, when William deserted her. This petition, filed during the October term 1817, in Washington County, orders William to appear at Potosi on the first Monday in June of 1818. In a later issue (June 7, 1820) John BRICKEY, an attorney, informed the public he was moving his practice to Boonville.

Ann M. CROSS, by her next friend, Isreal M'GREADY vs Joseph CROSS- This petition was filed during the October term 1817 in Washington County, and alleged Ann and Joseph were married on June 30, 1808, at Navy Island. Ann also claimed Joseph left her and the children on September 25, 1815. He was ordered to appear on the first Monday of the July term 1818 to answer the charges.

Vol. 10, No. 499, Apr 24, 1818. NOTICE- I will pay no debts of my wife, Mary Ann, who has left...Isaac COTTLE, Lower Cuivre, April 13, 1818.

Vol. 10, No. 504, May 15, 1818. NOTICE- Whereas my wife, Edy has without just cause or provocation, has forsaken bed and board...Kinchan CARTER, Alton, Illinois.

NOTICE- I will pay no debts of her (Hannah) contracting...Wm. PATERSON, May 14, 1818.

Vol. 10, No. 505, June 5, 1818. NOTICE- Whereas my wife Mary has left my bed and board...And. PORTER, St. Chas. Co., June 3, 1818.

NOTICE- I hereby forewarn all persons from trusting her (Sary) on my account. John STEWART, May 29, 1818.

Vol. 10, No. 516, Aug 21, 1818. NOTICE- ...not responsible for her (Elizabeth) debts. Wm. STEWART, August 21, 1818.

Vol. 11, No. 528, Oct 9, 1818. NOTICE-Whereas my wife Lucinda has willfully separated herself from me and is no longer under my care and protection...Edward PURSELL, St. Chas. Co., Oct 1, 1818.

NOTICE- Whereas my consort, Nelly has left me and her children in connection with one Joseph BEAUCHAMP; she being wholly directed by him as appears from their conduct...Wm. THOMSON, St. Cas. Co., September 19, 1818.

Vol. 11, No. 547, Mar 24, 1819. NOTICE- Whereas my consort has left my bed and board without lawful or just cause...John EDDS, Franklin Co., March 15, 1819.

Vol. 11, No. 565, July 28, 1819. NOTICE-...I forewarn the public from crediting of harboring my wife Lercille, formerly Lercille ORNOOCE, who has left me. Joseph LEMAN.

Vol. 11, No. 569, Aug 25, 1819. NOTICE- Know all men by these present that I, Jas. FORESTER, do forewarn all persons from trading or trafficking with my wife Mary, she having left...Jefferson Co., Aug. 11, 1819.

Vol. 11, No. 570, Sept 1, 1819. Elizabeth BLAINE, by her next friend, Daniel DUNKLIN vs Silas BLAINE- Elizabeth appeared before Nathaniel Beverly TUCKER, Presiding Judge, Washington County Circuit Court, and stated Silas left more than two years prior to the filing of this petition. Silas ordered to appear on the third Monday of the November term 1819.

Vol. 12, No. 577, September 22, 1819. NOTICE- I refuse to pay any debts of her (Eliza) contracting. Joseph DODIER, St. Louis.

Vol. 12, No. 583, Dec 1, 1819. NOTICE- I will not from this date pay any debts of her (Elizabeth) contracting. John KEITHLEY. St. Chas., Nov. 26, 1819.

Vol. 12, No. 585, Dec 15, 1819. NOTICE- Whereas my wife Phoebe GRIST, alias SMITH, has left my bed and board with a man named CARPENTER on July 10, 1819...John GRIST. St. Louis. December 10, 1819.

Vol. 12, No. 590, Jan 19, 1820. NOTICE- I am determined to pay no contracts or debts, she (Eulalie) having left my bed and board. John PAULET, Carondelet.

Vol. 12, No. 616, July 19, 1820. NOTICE- I will pay no debts of my wife Mary...Francois DEROIN.

Vol. 13, No. 644, Jan 31, 1821. NOTICE- My wife Elizabeth who has left my bed and board intends to go to Ste. Genevieve with her half-brother, John ROBINSON and buy items on credit in an attempt to ruin me. Michael HART, Ste. Genevieve Co., December 31, 1820.

Vol. 13, No. 654, Apr 11, 1821. NOTICE- I caution all persons not to trust her (Catherine) on my account. John MEARA, St. Louis.

Vol. 13, No. 655, Apr 18, 1821. NOTICE-...I am determined not to pay any debts of her (Hester) contracting. John CRISWELL.

Abraham JOHNSTON vs Hannah JOHNSTON- Hannah was ordered to appear during the next term of court, Franklin County, to answer the charge of desertion.

Vol. 13, No. 662, June 6, 1821. Whereas my husband Edward M'GINNIS, a carpenter by trade, has been absent from me for about one year, and I have reason to believe he is in the neighborhood of the Ohio River...Margaret M'GINNIS.

Vol. 14, No. 696, Jan 30, 1822. I do hereby forewarn all Persons from harboring my wife, Diannah and child, under penalty of the law...W.E.D. WINES.

NOTICE- All persons are cautioned against trading of selling on credit in my name to Emily, my wife. Paulet DEJARDIN, St. Louis.

PETITIONS HEARD BY
THE LEGISLATURE AND SUPREME COURT
1837 - 1849

Joseph HAMILTON vs Rebecca HAMILTON- This petition was sent from Ripley County, and was granted January 31, 1837.

Joab MOBERLEY vs Sally MOBERLEY- Sally was the former Sally KENELY before her marriage. This petition was granted on February 6, 1837.

D.W. REINHART vs Nancy REINHART- This petition was granted in 1838.

Elizabeth Permelia LIPSCOMB, late Elizabeth Permelia NOWLIN, requested the legislature for a divorce from Wade LIPSCOMB, charging the lower courts had been manipulated by her husband. A divorce was granted on January 29, 1839, and Elizabeth was given custody of their daughter, Lucy Ann.

Jane RICHARDS vs John RICHARDS- Jane, of Cape Girardeau County, asked that the law requiring a two year wait before filing for divorce be waived. This was done on February 16, 1841.

Polly Jane BOTTS vs Seth BOTTS- Polly asked that the law requiring a two year wait before filing for divorce in the case of abandonment be waived as Seth had committed a felony. Polly sent her request from Macon County. Approved February 16, 1841.

John THOMPSON vs Francis (JACKSON) THOMPSON- This petition, submitted on October 29, 1842, was filed on the grounds Francis and her father had committed fraud. John claimed eight to ten days after they were married, on January 25, 1838, John discovered Francis was pregnant by another man. John immediately returned her to her father's house, where her son was born the following April. John filed his petition for divorce with the legislature because he did not want to be further humiliated by filing in his home county of Marion.

Drucilla (WELDON) AUSTIN vs Richard AUSTIN- In this petition sent from Howard County, Drucilla's guardian, John HARVEY claimed he did not learn of the marriage until after the fact. John claimed Drucilla and Richard only lived together a few weeks before Richard returned to his home in Randolph County. John had filed this petition after learning Richard intended to file suit against John for control of Drucilla's money and property after she comes of age. This petition was heard on December 23, 1842.

Luthena LANCASTER vs Joseph LANCASTER- Luthena claimed she married Joseph on May 7, 1841, at the age of 15. Joseph returned her to her father's house on August 10, 1841, and left her there. She also accused him of becoming a habitual drunkard. When this petition was submitted to the legislature on December 26, 1842, from Lafayette County, Joseph was believed to be stationed at Fort Smith, Arkansas.

John LAKEY vs Rebecca (COX) LAKEY- John, a resident of Dade County, petitioned the legislature for a divorce as Rebecca was living at Hardeman County, Tennessee. Both parties agreed to the divorce when this petition was submitted in 1843.

William HARRIS vs Clarissa (OWNEY) HARRIS- This divorce was granted on January 7, 1847.

Elizabeth Ann NOELL, of Madison County, requested permission to petition for a divorce even though her husband, William, had not been gone two years. Approved February 17, 1843.

On February 23, 1843, Luthena LANCASTER, formerly Luthena RUBEY was finally given permission to sue for divorce on February 23, 1843, in Jackson County.

Charlotte E. YOUNT of Scott County, asked for permission to sue for divorce without waiting the required two years. Her husband was not named. Approved February 24, 1843.

Elizabeth HEREFORD vs James HEREFORD- This divorce petition was submitted from Scotland County, and was granted February 25, 1843.

Robert H. REED vs Mary REED- Robert of Marion County, filed suit against the former Mary LETTERAL, of Indiana, on the grounds of desertion. Petition granted on February 27, 1843.

Relief STEWARD vs John L. STEWARD- Relief filed her petition from Lincoln County, and was given permission to marry again when this divorce was granted on February 27, 1843.

Cynthia HAWKINS vs George HAWKINS- When this divorce was granted on March 12, 1843, Cynthia's maiden name of ZUMWALT was restored.

John LYNCH vs Elizabeth LYNCH- This petition was heard on October 29, 1843. In it John claimed that after the death of his first wife, he had married Elizabeth FOWLER. Soon after, she became abusive to John and his five children, making life unbearable. John had petitioned the Platte County Circuit Court for a divorce after he and Elizabeth had been separated for two years, but that petition was denied, forcing John to appeal to the legislature.

Warden Congreve JACKSON vs Elizabeth JACKSON- This petition was filed by William of Howard County, because when he married Elizabeth CROCKETT, of Chariton County in May of 1844, Elizabeth had considered it a jest, and not an actual ceremony. A divorce was granted on January 24, 1845.

Nelson ROP vs Eliza Jane ROP- Nelson claimed he and Eliza Jane WASH were married on October 9, 1835. They later separated because in Nelson's opinion, Eliza did not "conduct herself in a manner befitting a wife, as she refused to follow orders". This petition was submitted on January 30, 1845, from Morgan County, but was denied.

Millie OWENS vs William OWENS- In this petition from Shannon County, William was accused of leaving six years earlier, with his whereabouts unknown when the petition was heard on November 5, 1844. Millie asked that her petition only be granted if it would not affect the legitimacy of her children. The divorce was granted on January 24, 1845.

William BOYD vs Huldah BOYD- William claimed he had married Huldah EPPERSON on March 11, 1810, in Tennessee, but she deserted him on April 15, 1844. This petition was sent from Greene County on November 21, 1844.

Christopher KLANE vs Johanna KLANE- This petition was submitted from Jefferson County on December 7, 1844, on the grounds Johanna had left Christopher on August 1, 1844.

Joseph GIBSON vs Ursella GIBSON- This petition was sent from Van Buren County in 1844.

Isaac BRYSON vs Margaret L. BRYSON- Sent from Pike County, Isaac claimed his wife, the former Margaret L. LOVE, had deserted him. Divorce granted on February 24, 1845.

Frederick ARRENT vs Sarah ARRENT- Frederick claimed he had married Sarah HAWKE in March of 1824, in Hampshire County, Virginia. They separated in June of the following year. He also stated in his deposition given before John TERRILL, J. P. of Chariton County, that he moved to Missouri in 1839. This petition was granted on March 13, 1845.

Elizabeth T. (WALLACE) HINEMAN vs James HINEMAN- This petition was sent from Ste. Genevieve County on November 7, 1846. Elizabeth claimed she and James were married November 27, 1840, and later had two children, Elizabeth Ann, age 4, and Artemesia Avington Hineman, age 1, when the petition was filed. When her testimony was taken, Elizabeth also stated James had made it a habit to stay gone for months at a time, returning only to have his clothes patched, and to take what provisions Elizabeth had managed to accumulate. Elizabeth's two brothers, James and Wyat WALLACE, made sworn statements that Elizabeth's deposition was true.

Elias BURRIS vs Melinda BURRIS- This couple was married in July of 1842. Melinda left him on March 1, 1846 when Elias was ill, and returned to her father, David BURRIS, in southern Missouri. In an attempt to reconcile, Elias moved with Melinda to her brother James' home in Texas. When Elias wanted to return to Missouri, Melinda refused. He later learned Melinda and her lover, William WARDEN, had planned to steal his team and wagon and flee to the Choctaw Nation. Elias petitioned the legislature for a divorce because he had spent all his money following Melinda from place to place, so he was unable to pay the cost of a divorce in the Van Buren County Circuit Court. This petition was sent in November of 1846.

Pauline D. TAYLOR vs J. Ben TAYLOR- This petition for divorce was submitted on January 20, 1847. Pauline claimed Ben left her at the home of one of his friends without providing for her support. Pauline also stated Ben had gone to Liberty, Clay County, where he spent eight to ten days gambling and drinking until he was driven from there. This divorce was granted on February 2, 1847.

Jane WATT vs John WATT- This divorce was granted August 24, 1848.

Sarah Jane (TULLY) VAN GRAILMAN'S petition was granted February 13, 1849 (husband not named).

Elvira MOORE vs Edward H. MOORE- This petition was granted on February 13, 1849.

Eugene DEPRE vs Louisa Ann DEPRE, formerly Louisa Ann PAPEN- Petition granted February 22, 1849.

Sarah MAYO vs Peyton R. MAYO- This petition was finalized on February 23, 1849.

Sarah G. ODELL vs Thomas R. ODELL- Sarah sent her petition from Johnson County, and it was granted on February 24, 1849.

Nancy HIGH vs Randolph HIGH- Granted on February 24, 1849, this divorce petition had been sent from St. Clair County.

John W. PAYTON vs Pauline PAYTON- Sent from Grundy County, this petition was granted on February 27, 1849.

John B. KELSICK vs Margaret KELSICK- This petition was granted in March of 1849.

Britton A. HILL vs Melinda HILL- Granted March 2, 1849.

Mary WILSON vs Benjamin WILSON- This petition was submitted by Mary, who lived in Ste. Genevieve County. It was granted March 2, 1849.

Isabella ATTERBURY vs Zephaniah ATTERBURY- In her petition, Isabella stated she was formerly Isabella JAY. This petition was granted March 3, 1849.

Martha ABRAMS vs Benjamin ABRAMS- In her petition sent from Scotland County, Martha requested her name be changed to Martha CLEMMONS. The divorce was granted on March 3, 1849.

Sarah E. CHANEY vs Richard F. CHANEY- When she sent her petition for divorce from Boone County, Sarah asked that her name be restored to Sarah E. PEMBERTON. This petition was granted March 5, 1849.

William CATES vs Mary Ann CATES- In his petition, William stated he had married Mary Ann ROUTH, but that after she left him for another man he assumed she had gotten a divorce, so he later married Nancy HILL. He sent his petition to the legislature asking that he be granted a divorce from Mary, and that his marriage to Nancy be legalized from Ray County. Both requests were granted on March 5, 1849.

Margaret RIDGEWAY vs Thomas RIDGEWAY- This petition was sent from Lewis County. When it was granted on March 5, 1849, Margaret's surname was changed to CROOKS.

Robert SNELL vs Elizabeth SNELL, formerly Elizabeth SIMPSON- This petition was granted March 5, 1849.

Thomas J. DOOLIN vs Levina DOOLIN, formerly Levina NUTT - This petition was granted March 5, 1849.

Bartley W. GORIN vs Mary E. GORIN- March 5, 1849.

Mary GREEN vs Ansel GREEN- In her petition, sent from Platte County, Mary asked that her maiden name of Mary MARKLAND be restored. Her divorce petition was granted on March 6, 1849.

Nancy (GIBSON) FRANKLIN vs Josiah FRANKLIN- This divorce petition was sent from Knox County, and was granted on March 6, 1849.

Levina CLARK vs James CLARK- In her petition for divorce, Levina stated she was the former Levina MASON, and that she was a resident of Ste. Genevieve County. A divorce was granted on March 6, 1849.

James DAVIS vs Wyrinda DAVIS- When this petition was filed, James claimed his wife was the former Wyrinda STEEL. The divorce was granted on March 6, 1849.

William C. FAWKES vs Mary FAWKES- William, of Clinton County, filed this petition for divorce against his wife, the former Mary STEPHENSON, of Randolph County in 1848. It was granted March 6, 1849.

Susanna PERKINS vs John PERKINS- This petition was sent from Moniteau County, and was granted on March 6, 1849.

Nancy SNEIGER vs Robert SNEIGER- Sent from Pike County, this petition was finalized on March 6, 1849.

Robert ROLAND vs Ulrica ROLAND- Petition granted Mar. 6, 1849.

William T. PAGE vs Lelisa Ann PAGE- William sent his petition for a divorce from his wife, the former Lelisa Ann TETER. It was granted on March 7, 1849.

Jemima ARMFIELD vs Jonathan ARMFIELD- In her petition, granted on March 8, 1849, Jemima stated she was the former Jemima LINVILLE.

Nancy (CAMPELL) VIATELL vs Jackson VIATELL- A divorce was granted on March 8, 1849.

Martha Frances HERRIMAN vs Charles HERRIMAN- In this petition, Mary asked for custody of their child, which was granted on March 10, 1849.

Jane INGRAM vs George D. INGRAM- This petition was sent from Callaway County, and was granted on March 10, 1849.

Nancy SMITH vs Isaac SMITH- In her petition, sent from Ray County, Nancy stated she was the former Nancy MAXWELL. This petition was granted on March 10, 1849.

Susan SHELTON vs William H. SHELTON- Granted March 10, 1849.

William PAYNE vs Elvira PAYNE- William, of Daviess County, claimed his wife was the former Elvira JOHNSON. Petition granted March 10, 1849.

Nancy REINHART vs Davis W. REINHART- Petition granted March 12, 1849.

Clayton TIFFIN vs Julia G. (CROW) TIFFIN- This petition was sent from St. Louis, and was granted March 12, 1849.

John HARRIS vs Elizabeth HARRIS- Final March 12, 1849. Susan PILE vs John PILE- Granted on March 12, 1849.

Nancy BRYAN vs Benjamin B. BRYAN- This petition was sent from Cole County, and was finalized on March 12, 1849.

Mary Jane FERGUSON vs Moses C. FERGUSON- Mary stated in her petition, sent from Saline County, that she was the former Mary McMAHAN. This petition was granted March 12, 1849.

Ann LONG vs George LONG- Granted March 12, 1849.

Thomas KIMBLE vs Caroline (nee MIDDLETON) KIMBLE- Granted March 12, 1849.

John ECKLER vs Sophia Lee ECKLER- Final March 12, 1849.

Katherine HARGIS vs Hardin HARGIS- When Katherine sent her petition from Sullivan County, she asked that her maiden name of CHAMBERS be restored, which was done when the petition for divorce was granted on March 12, 1849.

Louise LOGAN vs William LOGAN- This petition was sent from Mercer County, and in it Louise asked that her maiden name of RUSSELL be restored. This was granted March 17, 1849.

Juliet Maria REYNOLDS vs Loring H. REYNOLDS- In her petition, sent from Howard County, Juliet stated her maiden name was Juliet Maria CLEVELAND. This petition was granted Mar 24, 1849.

The Missouri Supreme Court also ruled on a number of divorces.

Marianne STOKES vs William STOKES- This petition was sent from St. Louis County in 1832. Marianne claimed she and William were married in 1802, and in 1807 the couple separated by mutual consent. William then lived with Ann SMITH in England from 1809 to 1818. He and Ann later emigrated to America, finally settling in St. Louis. Marianne left England in 1816 for France. Petition dismissed as the separation had been by mutual choice.

In 1833, the Court overruled the divorce granted to Elvira (FRY) GENTRY which had been granted by the legislature.

Mildred D. LEWIS vs Samuel LEWIS- This divorce was the first granted on the grounds of mental indignities. Final in 1838.

Patrick RYAN vs Mary Ann RYAN- Petition denied when it was proven Patrick had committed adultery with Emily MONTAGUE, and others not named.

Martha S. CHEATHAM vs Joseph B. CHEATHAM- After their marriage in Saline County on September 11, 1846, Samuel threatened to shoot Martha. He also accused her of adultery before leaving November 22, 1846. This petition was denied because it was not stated in the petition if these events occurred in Missouri or elsewhere.

Martin N. NAGEL vs Parthena NAGEL- The Court denied this petition filed from Clinton County in 1848, because neither party was innocent.

DUNCAN vs DUNCAN- The decision of the lower court was reversed by the Supreme Court.

O'BRYAN vs O'BRYAN- This petition had been filed in Cooper County on December 6, 1847. Witnesses for the plaintiff were Caleb, Dixon, John L. and Jordan O'BRYAN, brothers of the plaintiff, Jordan O. TAYLOR, Mrs. L. ELLIOT, Simon LEWIS, and Elizabeth SAUNDERS. The Court also found the defendant had committed adultery with Thomas SAUNDERS, John SAUNDERS, and Eli CUTHRELL, and upheld the lower court's decision to grant the divorce.

THE MISSOURI REPUBLICAN
1822 - 1850

Vol. 1, No. 5, Apr 17, 1822. Susan EDSON, by her next friend, Pascal ENOS vs Casper R. EDSON- This petition was filed during the February term 1822, and ordered Casper to answer the complaint on the first Monday of the June term, 1822, in St. Louis County Circuit Court.

Vol. 1, No. 37, Nov 27, 1822. CAUTION- My wife Nancy has left my bed and board...Toussaint COUSENEAU, November 19, 1822.

A notice of desertion was published by Rebecca EATON of Detroit concerning the whereabouts of her husband, Moses R. EATON, who left in December of 1821 for Illinois or Missouri.

Vol. 1, No. 51, Mar 5, 1823. NOTICE- I am not responsible for the debts of my wife Winifred...Elisha E. BROOK.

Vol. 2, No. 64, June 4, 1823. Joseph JACKSON vs Mary JACKSON- Mary was ordered to appear on the first day of the next term Pike County Circuit Court to answer the petition.

Vol. 2, No. 68, July 2, 1823. NOTICE- The public are hereby forewarned against trusting or harboring my wife, formerly Emily BEYON...Charles MOJIN.

Vol. 2, No. 74, Aug 13, 1823. Sarah GARNER, by her next friend, Hugh McDERMID vs Thruston GARNER- Thruston was ordered to appear on the second Monday, November term 1823, at Pickney, Montgomery County.

Vol. 2, No. 94, Dec 31, 1823. Frances M. LEWIS vs John LEWIS- This petition was filed in St. Louis, and again on December 27, 1824.

Vol. 3, No. 143, Dec 20, 1824. NOTICE- The public are hereby cautioned against trusting anyone on my account...Antoine CHOQUETTE, November 20, 1824.

Vol. 3, No. 149, Jan 31, 1825. NOTICE- My wife Polly has left my bed and board...Noah PAINE, January 26, 1825.

Vol. 3, No. 152, Feb 21, 1825. Nancy METCALF, by her next friend, H. HENDRICK vs Washington METCALF- Washington was ordered to appear during the April term 1825, at Herculaneum, Jefferson County.

Vol. 4, No. 170, June 27, 1825. Anna WELCH vs Thomas W. WELCH- Filed during the March term 1825, this petition ordered Thomas to appear on the fourth Monday in July of 1825 in St. Louis.

Hester CRISWELL, by her next friend, William KIDD vs John CRISWELL- John was ordered to appear on the fourth Monday of the July term 1825, in St. Louis.

Vol. 4, No. 202, Feb 2, 1826. NOTICE- ...no man shall harbour her her to do midwifery without settling with me for it. Thomas BENTON.

Vol. 4, No. 205, Feb 23, 1826. ELOPEMENT- Eloped from my bed and board on the 14th inst., my wife Elizabeth Ann...George ALLEN, February 20, 1826.

Vol. 5, No. 214, Apr 27, 1826. NOTICE- Whereas my wife Lydia has left my bed and board...Daniel HIBLER, St. Louis County, April 24, 1826.

Vol. 5, No. 229, Aug 10, 1826. Harriet PHELAN, by her next friend, Christopher C. EASTON vs James C. PHELAN- This petition was filed in Pike County on the grounds James deserted his wife in December of 1833 at Clarksville. Harriet later moved to Bowling Green where she filed for divorce. James ordered to appear on the first Thursday of the October term 1826.

Vol. 5, No. 249, Nov 2, 1826. Nancy SCHWIMMER, by her solicitor, Robert W. WELLS vs John SWIMMER- Married on February 26, 1822, John left March 24, 1824. He was ordered to appear on the first Thursday of the following February term in Bowling Green, Pike County.

Vol. 5, No. 256, Feb 22, 1827. Eliza PEARSON, by her next friend, EDWARD HALL vs Daniel PEARSON- In this petition, filed in St. Charles County during the November term 1826, Eliza claimed she was married on October 12, 1819, in St. Louis County, and had one child before Daniel left in November of 1821. She also stated that she and her child moved to St. Charles County in 1824. Daniel was ordered to appear on March 1, 1827 to answer charges.

Vol. 6, No. 277, Sept 20, 1827. Eleanor THARP vs William THARP- In her petition for maintenance, Eleanor stated she and William were married in 1806. In January of 1825, William left her and the children. Eleanor also requested in her petition that William be ordered to end his threats to hold the administrix of her mother's estate answerable for money paid to Eleanor.

Vol. 6, No. 303, Dec 20, 1827. Mary NASON, by her next friend (not named) vs Culbert NASON- After their marriage in 1821, Culbert was accused of leaving the state in November of 1823. This petition ordered Culbert to appear in St. Louis County Circuit Court on the first Monday of the next term.

Vol. 7, No. 318, Apr 29. 1828. Rosanna TRENT, by her next friend, William DRENAN vs William TRENT- Married about ten years prior to the filing of this petition in Jefferson County, Rosanna claimed she and William lived together about five years before he left her and their two children.

Vol. 7, No. 326, June 17, 1828. NOTICE- ...I hereby forewarn all persons from trusting of harbouring my wife Elizabeth...Benjamin BANISTER, June 14, 1828.

Vol. 7, No 340, Sept 23, 1828. NOTICE- ...my wife Agnes LASLEY as she has wickedly disregarded the solemnity of her vows and the sanctity of the marriage state. Alexander LASLEY, Franklin Co., September 6, 1828.

Vol. 7, No. 345, Oct 28, 1828. Elizabeth STEELE, by her next friend, Richard KERR vs Robert STEELE- Elizabeth stated she and Robert were married September 15, 1803. Robert left her and their five children in November of 1814. Robert was ordered to appear on the first Thursday of the next term at Bowling Green, Pike County.

Vol. 8, No. 369, Apr 7, 1829. CAUTION- This is to caution all persons from crediting my wife Martha who has thought proper to abscond...St. Louis, Richard DOWLING, April 4, 1829.

Vol. 8, No. 370, Apr 28, 1829. Eulalie ARMSTRONG vs John ARMSTRONG- This petition was filed during the March term 1829, in St. Louis County. John was accused of leaving in July of 1824, for parts unknown. Eulalie claimed she and John had been married for eleven years when she filed her petition. John ordered to appear on the fourth Monday in July.

Vol. 8, No. 377, June 9, 1829. CAUTION- All persons are hereby cautioned from trusting Rose AIGUIES, my wife, in my name...Louis Joseph JEAUVOIVE.

Vol. 8, No. 380, June 30, 1829. Ardelia WOODBRIDGE, by her next friend, Martial COTTLE vs William W. WOODBRIDGE- Married September 1, 1825, William deserted Ardelia on April 27, 1827, according to this petition which was filed in Lincoln County on June 23, 1829. William was ordered to appear on the second Monday in October.

Vol. 8, No. 394, Oct 6, 1829. CAUTION- Be it known to all persons that my wife, Elizabeth HENRY hath, without any just cause, made her elopement...Malcolm HENRY, Sept 24, 1829.

Vol. 8, No. 395, Oct 13, 1829. Morris LADUKE vs Eulalie (LAS-AGE) LADUKE- Filed in St. Charles Circuit Court, October term, this petition ordered Eulalie to appear on the first Monday in February on 1830.

Vol. 8, No. 402, Dec 1, 1829. Nancy SIMMONS, Wm. M. SIM-MONS- Filed in St. Louis during the July term 1829, Nancy claimed in her petition that she and William were married August 5, 1821, and after they had two children, William left in 1824. Nancy also told the Court that she and the children were being supported by her father, Samuel HIBLER, when she filed.

Vol. 8, No. 415, Mar 2, 1830. NOTICE- Whereas my wife Polly CARROLL has left my bed and board...John B. CARROLL, St. Louis, February 25, 1830.

Vol. 8, No. 416, Mar 16, 1830. JOHN JAMISON vs Mary JAMI-SON- Filed in Pike County during the February term 1830, this petition stated John and Mary were married September 1, 1824, and Mary left four months later to move with her father to another part of the country. Mary was ordered to appear on the first Thursday of June.

Vol. 9, No. 421, Apr 20, 1830. NOTICE- I hereby forewarn all persons from trusting or protecting my wife, Hannah W. FLETCH-ER...D. FLETCHER, St. Louis, April 11, 1830.

Ann CHESLEY, by her next friend, Nancy BURGET vs Alexander

C. CHELSEY- In this petition filed in Perry County during the March term 1830, Alexander was accused of deserting Ann six years earlier.

Vol. 10, No. 468, Mar 15, 1831. NOTICE- Whereas my wife Meeky has left my bed and board...James SCOTT, St. Louis Co., March 14, 1831.

Vol. 10, No. 480, May 31, 1831. NOTICE- All persons are hereby warned from trusting or giving credit to my wife Polly MEYERS...Jacob MEYERS, St. Charles, May 27, 1831.

Vol. 10, No. 481, June 6, 1831. Genevieve DETAILLE vs Pierre DETAILLE- This petition was filed in March of 1831, and claimed the couple was married in St. Louis in 1817. Pierre was ordered to appear on the fourth Monday of November, 1831, to answer the charge that he deserted Genevieve in 1820.

Sarah Ann B. ELDER vs Augustine W. ELDER- When this petition was filed in St. Louis in 1831, Augustine was accused of deserting Sarah six months after they were married in 1827.

Julian Ann GRANJEAN vs Abraham F. GRANJEAN- Filed in St. Louis, this petition claimed that after their marriage in 1821, Abraham continuously abused and ill treated Julian before finally deserting her.

Vol. 10, No. 500, Oct 18, 1831. Margaret BROWN, by her next friend, Wm. KERR vs Henry S. BROWN- This petition for divorce was filed during the September term 1831 in Pike County. Margaret claimed she and Henry were married in July of 1814 in St. Charles, where they lived until 1820. They then moved to Pike County, where they resided until February of 1828, at which time Henry left her and the four children. Henry was accused of living in the province of Texas with another woman when the petition was filed. He was ordered to appear in Court on the fourth Monday in January of 1832.

Vol. 11, No. 525, Apr 10, 1832. Elizabeth GAY vs David GAY- Filed in St. Louis during the March term 1832, this petition accused David of deserting Elizabeth and their child in 1825. David was required to appear on the fourth Monday in July of 1832 to answer charges.

Vol. 11, No. 535, June 19, 1832. NOTICE- Whereas my wife Nancy O. CALVERT has left my bed and board... Benson CALVERT, June 15, 1832.

Vol. 12, No. 707, June 26, 1834. NOTICE- This is to warn all persons from contracting any debts with my wife, Theodore...Noah C. WILLIS, June 23, 1834.

Vol. 12, No. 723, Aug 22, 1834. Louisa BURK vs William BURK- This petition was filed during the July term 1834 in St. Louis County. William was accused of ill treating Louisa before he finally left her and their infant daughter two years earlier. William was ordered to appear on the fourth Monday of November.

Vol. 12, No. 724, Aug 26, 1834. Hannah FLETCHER vs Daniel FLETCHER- Daniel was accused of deserting her and their child four years earlier. This petition required Daniel to appear on the first day of the November term.

Vol. 13, No. 770, Feb 6, 1835. NOTICE- Whereas my wife Nancy HENSLEY, and youngest child have left my bed and board...William HENSLEY, Franklin County.

Vol. 13, No. 787, Apr 3, 1835. Margaret M. JAMESON, by her solicitor, Mr. LOWRY vs Joseph JAMESON- Joseph was ordered to appear in Court in St. Louis on the first day of the next term. Joseph was charged with deserting Margaret and their two children in 1833.

Vol. 13, No. 792, Apr 21, 1835. NOTICE- Whereas my wife Agnes PROUHET has left my bed and board...S. PROUHET, River des Peres, St. Louis Co.

Vol. 14, No. 825, July 16, 1835. NOTICE- As I hear that my husband Francis W. BOLGIANO is mortgaging my lands laying in the counties of Quincy, Adams, and Hancock, Illinois, this is to inform all persons...Mary Jane BOLGIANO.

Vol. 14, No. 826, July 18, 1835. Frederick KLUCK vs Elizabeth KLUCK- Filed in Jefferson County during the July term 1833, this petition accuses Elizabeth of living in open adultery, She was ordered to appear on the first day of the next term to answer charges.

Vol. 14, No. 831, Aug 1, 1835. NOTICE- Whereas my wife Martha has left my bed and board...William BROWN.

Lucy HARRIS vs John HARRIS- Citing bigamy as the grounds for a divorce, this petition alleges John already had a wife when he and Lucy were married. He deserted Lucy in 1832, and moved in with yet another woman, to whom he pretended to be married. John

ordered to appear in Court on the second Monday of the November term 1835, in St. Louis.

Vol. 14, No. 837, Aug 15, 1835. NOTICE- Whereas my wife Rene RICHARD has left my bed and board...Noel RICHARD, St. Charles County, Aug 15, 1835.

Vol. 14, No. 895, Jan 2, 1836. Elvira G. SHADE, by her next friend, Reuben A. CARTER vs Jacob SHADE- This divorce petition was filed in Crawford County during the December term 1835. Jacob was ordered to appear in the April term to answer the complaint.

Vol. 15, No. 935, Apr 5, 1836. NOTICE- Whereas my wife Ellen, having left my bed and board without just cause...John MOONAY.

Vol. 15, No. 977, July 12, 1836. NOTICE- Whereas my wife Mary Victorine has left my bed and board...Emanuel De HODIAMONT, St. Louis, July 9.

Vol. 15, No. 994, August 20, 1836. NOTICE- Whereas my wife Ellen left my bed and board on the night of the 18th inst. ...John MURPHY.

Vol. 15, No. 1110, Jan 5, 1837. NOTICE- Whereas my wife Martha RAFFERTY did on the 24th instant, leave my bed and board...William RAFFERTY, Floresant, January 2.

Vol. 15, No. 1112, Jan 6, 1837. Peter G. SANDBERG vs Rosetta SANDBURG- This divorce petition was filed in St. Louis Circuit Court during the November term 1836. The petition stated Peter and Rosetta were married in New Orleans on May 8, 1825. In 1833, Rosetta left with another man for St. Louis. She was ordered to appear and answer the summons during the March term.

Vol. 15, No. 1143, Feb 12, 1837. This issue contained notices of two divorces granted by the Missouri Legislature, Jacob MOBLEY vs Sally MOBLEY, and Joseph HAMILTON vs Rebecca HAMILTON.

Vol. 15, No. 1198, Apr 21, 1837. James DAVIDSON vs Rhoda DAVIDSON- This petition was filed in Washington County during the March term 1837, and stated the couple was married in June of 1823. Rhoda was accused of eloping with another man in 1829, and going to Galena or Fever River Mines. She was ordered to appear on the second Monday of July in 1837.

Vol. 15, No. 1502, Mar 30, 1838. NOTICE-I do hereby forewarn all persons from trading, dealing, or trafficking with my wife Mary THURMAN...or preventing her return. Pleasant THURMAN.

Vol. 15, No. 1553, May 31, 1838. NOTICE- I hereby caution the public from trusting or harbouring my wife Bridget on my account...John TULLEY.

Vol. 15, No. 1572, Aug 3, 1838. Nancy GREGORY, by her next friend, Hezakiah GARRET vs Daniel GREGORY- In her petition, filed in Washington County, Nancy stated she and Daniel were married in October of 1834, but he left her two months later. She also stated she had lived in Washington County for twenty years.

TO THE PUBLIC- Whereas my wife Sarah BLANY has left my bed and board without just cause...John BLANY.

Vol. 15, No. 1618, Aug 12, 1838. Mary Jane BOLGIANO vs Francis W. BOLGIANO- Filed on June 1, 1838 in St. Louis County, this petition stated Mary and Francis were married in Baltimore on April 23, 1829. Francis was accused of being a habitual drunkard and of subjecting Mary to two years of cruel and barbarous treatment. Mary asked for custody of the couple's son, Francis A. BOLGIANO.

Vol. 15, No. 1619, Aug 14, 1838. NOTICE- Whereas my wife Catherine Jane DAVIS has left my bed and board without provocation...I will receive her if she will return to my house! John E. DAVIS.

TO THE PUBLIC- About May a year ago, I was married in the county of St. Louis to Betsy ALLEN- Since that time I have found out the said Betsy has another husband living and it is my intention to apply for a divorce on the grounds of the nullity of said marriage. I hereby forewarn all persons from giving her credit on my account. Samuel KINCAID.

Vol. 15, No. 1639, Sept 8, 1838. CAUTION- Whereas my wife Catherine has left my bed and board...Gabriel J. OBUCHON.

Vol. 15, No. 1706, Nov 30, 1838. Elizabeth D. MELLSAPS vs James MELLSAPS- When Elizabeth, the former Elizabeth. D. HIGGENBOTHAM, filed for divorce during the November term 1838, she stated she and James had been married thirteen years earlier. After living together for four years, Elizabeth and the children went to live with her father because Elizabeth felt James was intemperate in his habits. Elizabeth also claimed James then lived with a woman in Franklin County until he was indicted for the murder of Reuben OGLESBY, after which he fled to Texas.

Vol. 15, No. 1706, Nov 30, 1838. Permelia CHRISTMAN, by her next friend, Thomas SYDNOR vs William P. CHRISTMAN- Filed during the November term 1838, in Lincoln County, this petition stated the couple were married May 18, 1837. After William left her in August of 1837, Permelia went to live with her uncle, who supported her. William was ordered to appear in Court on the first Monday of the April term 1839.

Vol. 15, No. 1735, Jan 11, 1839. Ann HOLDERMAN vs Christopher HOLDERMAN- After they were married in 1811, the couple lived together for eighteen years before Christopher left, according to this petition filed in Jefferson County.

Vol. 15, No. 1785, Mar 15, 1839. NOTICE- Whereas my wife Theresa GINGRA has absconded herself from my bed without just cause...Pierre GINGRA, Justin GLOSCLAUDE, witness.

Vol. 15, No. 1961, Oct 11, 1839. NOTICE- The conduct of my wife Margaret MEBUS, late Margaret SCHIEACHER, of St. Louis, having constrained me to separate from her...I intend to apply to the Circuit Court of Madison County, Illinois, for a divorce. John MEBUS, Alton, Ill. October 7, 1839.

Vol. 15, No. 1976, Oct 29, 1839. Andile CAVENER vs James CAVENER- This petition, filed on September 27, 1839, in Madison County stated the couple were married December 18, 1835, and lived together until March 25, 1836. Andile also requested any claim James might make to the land she owned before her marriage, be disallowed. James was ordered to appear on the fourth Monday of the January term 1840, to answer the charges.

Vol. 15, No. 2073, Feb 20, 1840. Helen DARGE vs Joseph DARGE- After they were married on October 23, 1838, Joseph left Helen the following month.

Vol. 19, No. 2110, Apr 3, 1840. Joan KINDAL vs George KINDAL- In her petition, Joan claimed she and George were married on November 3, 1836. George was ordered to appear in Crawford County Circuit Court to answer the summons.

Vol. 19, No. 2305, Nov 13, 1840. NOTICE- My wife Prudence BEVERADGE, having left me for the second time ...W. BEVERADGE.

Vol. 19, No. 2272, Jan 22, 1841. TAKE NOTICE- My wife Jane left my house without just cause or provocation ...Wm. D. HICKMAN.

Vol. 20, No. 2452, Aug 20, 1841. John BROWN vs Katherine BROWN- John stated in his petition, filed July 19, 1841, in Jefferson County, that he and Katherine were married on August 20, 1839. He had claimed Katherine had deserted him.

Vol. 20, No. 2465, Sept 6, 1841. CAUTION- Whereas my wife Virginia has left...J. B. DUCHOQUETTE.

Vol. 20, No. 5607, Feb 17, 1842. NOTICE- My wife Lucile Le-CLAIR, having left my bed and board without just cause...Pierre LEVREMONT.

Vol. 20, No. 5614, Feb 25, 1842. NOTICE- My wife, born Sophia KRUSE in the district of Gronrae on the Seine...left me and five children on January 14th... Ran off with Henry BAMPENDAHL. Henry JUSTUS.

Vol. 20, No. 5647 Apr 5, 1842. Mary NEWBERRY vs Henry NEWBERRY- This divorce petition was filed in St. Louis Circuit Court on January 3, 1842. Henry was ordered by the Court to appear on the third Monday of the July term 1842, to answer charges.

Vol. 20, No. 5668, Apr 29, 1842. Elizabeth NEAL, by her next friend, Amos BURDYNE vs Litel NEAL- After this petition was filed in St. Charles County, Litel was ordered to appear on the 6th day of the following term.

Nancy JACKSON, by her next friend, Amos BURDYNE vs Jacob JACKSON- Filed on the grounds of desertion, Jacob was ordered to appear in the St. Charles County Circuit Court on the 6th day of the next term.

Vol. 21, No. 5677, May 10, 1842. Mary J. RIDDLE vs Abraham RIDDLE- After Mary filed her petition for divorce in St. Louis County, the Circuit Court ordered Abraham to appear on November 3, 1842, to answer the allegation of desertion.

Vol. 21, No. 5701, June 6, 1842. TO THE PUBLIC- Whereas my wife Spicey MAUPIN left my bed and board... Wilkerson MAUPIN, Franklin County, May, 1842.

Vol. 21, No. 5731, July 12, 1842. Hugh WHITE vs Emeline WHITE- The St. Louis County Circuit Court ordered Emeline to appear and answer the charge of desertion on the third Monday of the November term.

Vol. 21, No. 5749, Aug 2, 1842. Caroline M. WRIGHT vs Harrison WRIGHT- In her divorce petition, filed in Washington County during the June term, Caroline stated she and Harrison were married November 29, 1836 in Crawford County.

Vol. 22, No. 2894, Jan 19, 1843. Cornelius LAUDRIGAN vs Catherine LAUDRIGAN- This divorce petition was filed in St. Louis County on the grounds of desertion.

Vol. 22, No. 3003, May 25, 1843. Nicholas ARNST vs Rachel ARNST- Filed May 17, 1843, in St. Louis County on the grounds of desertion, this petition for divorce was continued to the November term 1843, when Rachel was ordered to appear.

Vol. 22, No. 3039, July 6, 1843. Elizabeth HOHNHOLIZ vs Henry HOHNHOLIZ- After this divorce petition was filed in St. Louis County, Henry was ordered to appear on the third Monday of the November term.

Vol. 22, No. 3072, Aug 14, 1843. Eliza GRAHAM vs Thomas GRAHAM- When Eliza filed for divorce in Washington County, she claimed she and Thomas were married in Mercer County, Pennsylvania on February 8, 1841.

Vol. 22, No. 3101, Oct 21, 1843. NOTICE- My wife, Mary Ann has left...is tall and slender with red hair, freckled, and has one tooth missing...John HILL.

Vol. 22, No. 3160, Nov 22, 1843. Mathias BECKER vs Elizabeth BECKER- Filed in St. Louis County on November 2, 1843, this publication notice ordered Elizabeth to appear on the third Monday of the April term 1844 to answer the charge.

Vol. 22, No. 3183, Dec 20, 1843. Sarah WINCHESTER vs James WINCHESTER- This petition for divorce was filed in New Madrid County.

Vol. 22, No. 3208, Jan 22, 1844. NOTICE- Whereas my wife Leonore FLOREZ has left my bed and board... Bernardine FLOREZ, St. Louis.

Vol. 23, No. 3258, Apr 22, 1844. NOTICE- My wife Adeline MELLOT has left my bed and board...I will pay no debts of her contracting from and after the 17th of the present month...She has gone, I believe to Prairie du Rocher, Randolph County, Illinois. Joseph MELLOT.

Vol. 23, No. 3265, Apr 30, 1844. NOTICE- Whereas my wife Ruth WEBB has left...Thomas H. WEBB, March 28, 1844.

Vol. 23, No. 3317, June 29, 1844. PUBLIC NOTICE- The public are hereby warned not to trust any person on my account as I will not pay any debts unless contracted by myself in person. C. STURN, Franklin County.

Vol. 23, No. 3339, July 25, 1844. Mary Ann ELLSWORTH vs Thomas ELLSWORTH- When Mary filed her petition for divorce in St. Louis County, she claimed she and the defendant were married in 1833. She also stated Thomas had left her on November 5, 1841. The Court ordered Thomas to appear on the third Monday of the November term.

Vol. 23, No. 3349, Aug 6, 1844. Mahala J. BEESON vs Elisha S. BEESON- Mary filed this petition in Clark County by her solicitor, John M. CHILDRESS. Mahala claimed she and Elisha were married on July 29, 1841, but that he left her the following February, claiming he had business in Ohio.

Vol. 23, No. 3483, Jan 14, 1845. NOTICE- All persons are hereby cautioned and forewarned against trusting my wife Elizabeth STEEL, on my account as I will pay no debts of her contracting...unless compelled by law. Henry L. STEEL, St. Ferdinand Twp., St. Louis.

Vol. 23, No. 3502, Feb 6, 1845. Polly ROUNDTREE vs Turner ROUNDTREE- After Polly filed her petition for divorce by her solicitor, Wm. PORTER, the Warren County Circuit Court ordered Turner to appear on the fourth Monday of the April term.

Vol. 23, No. 3523, Feb 27, 1845. NOTICE- Whereas my wife, Catherine, alias Kitt GILLMAN, formerly WALLITE, has left my bed and board without just cause...John GILLMAN, Jefferson County.

Vol. 24, No. 3642, July 19, 1845. NOTICE- To whom it may concern- On the 25th day of June 1845, in the Parish Court for the Parish and City of New Orleans, a judgment was ordered...that she be separated from the bed and board of defendant and also a separation of property and all monies or wealth. Mary C. LYONS, wife of Richard F. NICHOLS.

Vol. 24, No. 3653, Aug 7, 1845. Maria BATTLEBY vs John BATTLEBY- After this divorce petition was filed in St. Louis County, John was ordered by the Court to appear on the third Monday of the November term.

Vol. 24, No. 4838, Mar 4, 1846. NOTICE- Eloped from my bed and board on the last day of January 1846 my wife Edith RENNOLDS without my consent. I have repeatedly gone after her and kindly and affectionately implored her to return...but she only laughs and mocks my feeling invitation. William R. RENNOLDS, St. Louis Co.

Vol. 24, No. 4856, Mar 26, 1846. TO THE PUBLIC- On my return to this city I was surprised to find in the columns of the *Reveille* and other papers, signed by Mary COLE representing herself as my wife, and that I had left her and her child penniless and without clothes...I do not disavow having married this woman. Now I am prepared to prove her husband was still living at the time of our union. She was not left penniless, but brought home where it was in hopes she would remain. James COLE.

Vol. 25, No. 3963, Aug 10, 1846. Richard GILL vs Sarah GILL- This petition was filed in St. Louis County Circuit Court on July 21, 1846, on the grounds of desertion.

Vol. 25, No. 3981, Aug 31, 1846. Hiram SMITH vs Zilphie SMITH- In his divorce petition, Hiram claimed he had married Zilphie SIMPSON in September of 1838 in Randolph County, Arkansas, after which, they came to Missouri. She then left him in September of 1842, according to the petition. Zilphie was ordered to appear on the third Monday of November 1846, in Ste. Genevieve County to answer the charges.

Vol. 25, No. 3993, Sept 14, 1846. NOTICE- I forewarn the public from trusting my wife Mary, or any of the rest of my family under age...William STEWART, St. Louis.

Mary Ann LOVE vs William LOVE- This petition, filed in St. Louis County on grounds of desertion, ordered William to appear on the third Monday of the November term.

Vol. 25, No. 3997, Sept 18, 1846. NOTICE- Whereas my wife Elizabeth ADAMS, born Elizabeth FUCHS has left my bed and board...Haimos ADAMS.

Vol. 26, No. 13, Jan 16, 1847. Sarah GOLDSMITH vs Eugene GOLDSMITH- This divorce petition was filed in St. Louis County during the November term 1846, on the grounds of desertion. Eugene was ordered to appear in Court on the third Monday of the April term.

Vol. 26, No. 105, May 4. 1847. NOTICE- Whereas my wife Mary Ann Catherine BOOTH has left...Thomas BOOTH, St. Louis.

Vol. 26, No. 160, July 7, 1847. Sophia C. LANCASTER vs Aaron A. LANCASTER- This divorce petition was filed in St. Louis County.

Vol. 26, No. 178, July 29, 1847. Esther A. NUNNELLY vs Charles G. NUNNELLY- This petition for divorce was filed May 3, 1847, in St. Louis County. Charles was ordered to appear on the third Monday of the November term to answer the charge of desertion.

Robert B. RAWLINGS vs Alice RAWLINGS- Filed on July 19, 1847, in St. Louis on the grounds Alice had another husband still living at the time of her marriage to Robert. She was ordered to appear on the third Monday of the following November term.

Vol. 26, No. 303, Dec 20, 1847. Eli BAY vs Phoebe Ann BAY- This petition was filed in September of 1847, on the grounds of desertion, in Franklin County. Phoebe was ordered to appear on the fourth Monday of the March term 1848.

Vol. 27, No. 17, Jan 20, 1848. George AARON to Franky AARON- George filed his petition for divorce by R. W. SANDERS, his solicitor, in Warren County in the September term 1847. Franky was ordered to appear in the April term 1848.

Vol. 27, No. 19, Jan 22, 1848. NOTICE- Is hereby given, that my wife Mary Jane FUGATE of St. Louis has left my bed and board...Josiah FUGATE.

Vol. 27, No. 50, Feb 28, 1848. Henry F. CLARK vs Ann B. CLARK- This petition for divorce was filed in St. Louis County.

Vol. 27, No. 167, July 14, 1848. Adam JERANS vs Eliza JERANS- Citing desertion as grounds, this divorce petition was filed in St. Louis County.

Vol. 27, No. 190, Aug 10, 1848. NOTICE- Whereas my wife Sarah Jane FLETCHER has left my bed and board...took up with a man, George DAVIS...John G. FLETCHER, St. Louis.

Vol. 27, No. 269, Nov 10. 1848. Catherine ALIDER vs Moses John ALIDAR- After this petition was filed in St. Louis County, Moses was ordered to appear on the third Monday of the April term, or the bill would be taken as confessed.

Caution- All persons are hereby cautioned against trusting or trading with my wife Frances STEPHENSON on my account. Joseph STEPHENSON, St. Louis County, November 7, 1848.

Vol. 27, No. 292, Dec 8, 1848. Mary LEE vs James LEE- This divorce petition was filed in St. Louis County on September 12, 1848. James was ordered to appear the third Monday of the April term 1849.

Vol. 28, No. 25, Jan 30, 1849. Morris GEISLER vs Louise GEISLER- Morris filed his petition for divorce on the grounds of desertion on January 29, 1849. Louise was to answer the charges on the third Monday of the April term 1849, in St. Louis County Circuit Court.

James CONNELL vs Mary CONNELL- When James filed his divorce petition on January 29, 1849, he stated he and Mary were married in St. Louis in 1842. He accused Mary of adultery, leaving with John CROCKETT, and fleeing to Illinois.

Vol. 28, No. 36, Feb 12, 1849. John ELLSTON vs Elizabeth ELLSTON- This divorce petition was filed in Lincoln County in 1848.

Vol. 28, No. 42, Feb 18, 1849. Andrew J. DAWSON vs Sarah DAWSON- After hearing this petition for divorce, the St. Louis County Circuit Court ordered Sarah to appear on, or before the third Monday of the April term to answer the charges of adultery and desertion.

Vol. 28, No. 315, Jan 1, 1850. Ellen AUBUCHUM vs Hampton AUBUCHUM- This divorce petition was filed in St. Louis County during the November term 1849. Hampton was ordered to appear April 3, 1850.

Lucy ARMSTRONG vs Quinton ARMSTRONG- Quinton was charged with intemperance, desertion and adultery, and was ordered to appear the third Monday in April, 1849.

Vol. 29, No. 19, Jan 22, 1850. Alexander BALLENTINE vs Caroline BALLENTINE- Henry filed his petition against his wife, alias Caroline LANGWITH, formerly Caroline GRIFFITH in St. Louis County on the grounds she had committed adultery.

OTHER MISSOURI NEWSPAPERS
1819 - 1850

Missouri Intelligencer 23 Apr 1819: 1-1. Huldah DAVIS vs Harper C. DAVIS- Married on August 3, 1815, this couple lived together until September 4, 1816, when Harper left. He was ordered to appear on the second Monday of the July term 1819 to answer charges.

St. Louis Enquirer 13 Oct 1819 (no volume or issue number). NOTICE- Whereas my wife Elizabeth YARNELL, has left my bed and board...John YARNELL, St. Charles, September 25, 1819.

Missouri Intelligencer 12 Nov 1819: 1-27. NOTICE- I will not pay any debts of my wife Mary who has left without just cause. James ATTERBARY Sr., September 4, 1819.

Missouri Intelligencer 31 Dec 1819: 1-33. NOTICE- John M'COY will not pay any debts of his wife Elizabeth, who deserted him. Howard Co., December 3, 1819.

St. Louis Enquirer 10 May 1820: 3-166. Samuel SMILEY vs Dorotha SMILEY- Filed in St. Charles County on March 22, 1820, this petition charged Dorotha with leaving in October of 1817. She was ordered to appear on the first Monday of the July term 1820.

St. Louis Enquirer 14 June 1820: 1-194. NOTICE- My wife Celeste AMBROSE, formerly Celeste GIGUANE, having left my bed and board on the third inst. ...Louis Duberg AMBROSE, June 2, 1820.

Missouri Herald 10 June 1820: 1-45. Mary DAVIS, by her next friend (and brother), Charles WALL vs Isaac DAVIS- In her petition, Mary claimed she and Isaac were married March 2, 1813, and he left her in April of the same year. Isaac was ordered to appear at the Cape Girardeau County Circuit Court on the third Monday of August in 1820 to answer the petition.

Independent Patriot 12 May 1821: 1-25. Jane PATTERSON vs James PATTERSON- Jane filed her petition for divorce, filed in Cape Girardeau County, that she and James were married in 1796. He was accused of deserting her in 1817. James was ordered to appear on the first Monday of the August term 1820.

St Louis Enquirer 12 May 1821: 3-250. ELOPEMENT- Whereas my wife Elizabeth HAGGERTY has left my bed and board on the 7th April last past and is now leading a life of disgrace...Henry HAGGERTY, May 5.

The Missourian 13 June 1821: 1-51. Abraham JOHNSON vs Hannah JOHNSON- This petition for divorce, filed in Franklin County, accused Hannah of leaving in February of 1816.
    NOTICE- This is to forewarn all persons from harbouring or trusting my wife Hetty who has left... William HAGEN, St. Louis.

Independent Patriot 27 Oct 1821: 1-49. NOTICE- John MASSEY is not responsible for any debts of his wife (not named) who has left him. October 13, 1821.

The Missourian 22 Nov 1821: 2-74. A report of actions taken by the Missouri Legislature noted a divorce petition submitted by Joseph HUNTER was rejected.

The Missourian 6 Dec 1821: 2-76. John HUSKY vs Mary HUSKY- This divorce was granted by the legislature.
    A bill was also introduced requesting the marriage of John and Abigail FAREWILL be annulled, and was granted.

The Missourian 17 Jan 1822: 2-82. Catherine MEAD vs Isaac MEAD- Filed November 21, 1821, in Pike County on the grounds of desertion, this petition ordered Isaac to appear on the second Monday in March of 1822.

Independent Patriot 20 Jan 1822: 2-10. A report on legislative actions of the General Assembly of Missouri, included the granting of a divorce to John and Mary HUSKEY, and an annulment to John and Abigail FAREWELL appeared in this issue.

The Missourian 24 Jan 1822: 2-83. NOTICE- Whereas my wife Eliza has left my bed and board on the 17th inst. ...I also warn the people of Franklin where I suppose she has made her way. Thomas WILLS, St. Charles, January 17, 1822.

Missouri Gazette 20, Feb 1822: 14-699. NOTICE- I have lost my wife Elizabeth...Joseph HOGAN.

Missouri Intelligencer 2 Apr 1822: 3-35. NOTICE- I hereby forewarn all persons from trading with Theodotia CUNNINGHAM, in any respect, as I am determined to pay no debt of her contracting. William CUNNINGHAM.

The Missourian 4 July 1822: 2-102. NOTICE- Whereas my wife Louise has left my bed and board...Louis TANYON.

The Missourian 15 Aug 1822: 3-168. PUBLIC NOTICE- Whereas my wife Nancy has left my bed and board without good cause...Ira COTTLE, Monroe, July 23, 1822.

Independent Patriot 12 Oct 1822: 2-47. Elizabeth WILLIAMS vs William WILLIAMS- William was ordered to appear at the Madison County Circuit Court on the first Monday of the November term 1822 to answer the allegations made in this petition for divorce.

St. Louis Enquirer 15 Feb 1822: 3-345. NOTICE- ...The Public are hereby informed she (Ann) may now shift for herself. Michael ROBERTS

Independent Patriot 1 Mar 1823: 3-15. Elizabeth KEITH vs George KEITH- This divorce petition, filed in Scott County, ordered George to answer the summons on the second Monday in June of 1823.

Missouri Intelligencer 20 May 1823: 4-42. NOTICE- I will pay no debts of my wife Elizabeth who has left my bed and board...Roland SUTTON.

St. Louis Enquirer 21 June 1823: 3-26. Sarah FOSTER vs Dabney FOSTER- Filed in March of 1823, in Washington County on the grounds of desertion, this petition ordered Dabney to appear on the fourth Monday of July 1824.

Independent Patriot 9 Aug 1823: 3-37. NOTICE- Thomas H. GOALD will not assume the debts made by his wife Odeal. New Madrid County.

Independent Patriot 6 Sept 1823: 3-41. Harriet CROSS, by her next friend, Harvey LANE vs Joseph CROSS- This divorce petition was filed in Ste. Genevieve County. No grounds were cited.

Independent Patriot 4 Oct 1823: 3-29. Katherine WINDER published a notice seeking information as to the whereabouts of her husband, Samuel WINDER, who she claimed had deserted her.

Independent Patriot 11 Oct 1823: 3-47. NOTICE- I am determined not to be accountable for her (Elizabeth) contracts. John DUNN, Jackson, Mo., Sept 23, 1823.

St. Louis Enquirer 8 Nov 1823: 3-386. NOTICE- Whereas Nelly LeDUKE, my wife, has eloped from my bed and board...Morris LeDUKE, November 3, 1823.

St. Louis Enquirer 27 Dec 1823: 3-390. Victoire DABBIN, by her next friend, Baptiste MORAIN vs Pierre DABBIN- Filed during the October term 1823, this petition ordered Pierre to appear on the first Monday of the October term 1824, in St. Louis County.

Missouri Intelligencer 17 Apr 1824: 5-36. Lydia HINSON, by her next friend, Nicholas OWENS vs Griffin HINSON- After this petition was filed in Clay County, Griffin was ordered to appear on the second Monday of the July term 1824 at the home of John OWENS, where Court was to be held.

Missouri Intelligencer 1 May 1824: 5-38. NOTICE- ...as my wife Catherine has left my bed and board. William WILLIAMS, April 26, 1824.

St. Louis Enquirer 24 May 1824 3-22. NOTICE- I am determined to pay none of her (Keziah) debts of contracts in consequence of her elopement from my residence. William BOUNDS.

Missouri Intelligencer 17 July 1824: 5-49. William PATTON vs Martha PATTON- After this divorce petition was denied in Boone County, it was sent to the Missouri Legislature on an appeal.

Independent Patriot 14 Aug 1824: 4-59. Theodise BUTCHER, by her next friend, Charles GRIFFAR vs Benjamin BUTCHER- This petition, filed in Ste. Genevieve County was continued to the second Monday in the November term 1824, when Benjamin was ordered to appear.

St. Louis Enquirer 11 Dec 1824: 8-69. NOTICE- Whereas my wife Mary, did on the 26th day of October last, leave without just cause...Kinkead CALDWELL, Franklin Co., November 27, 1824.

Independent Patriot 8 Dec 1824: 5-3. Mary A. STIDGER, by her next friend, C. G. HOUTS vs William B. STIDGER- William was ordered by the Court to answer this summons on the first Monday in the February term 1825, in New Madrid County.

Independent Patriot 5 Feb 1825: 5- 14. NOTICE- Polly HEWS having absconded from my house without just cause...Teral HEWS, February 4, 1825.

Independent Patriot 19 Feb 1824: 5-16. NOTICE- The unlawful marriage between W. M. CHICK and Ann R. PULLAM was declared null and void.

Missouri Intelligencer 24 Mar 1826: 7-27. Amelia P. CAMPBELL, by her next friend, Nelson PEPPER vs David H. CAMPBELL- Amelia claimed she and David were married on August 26, 1821, but that David had been gone more than two years when the divorce petition was filed. He was ordered to appear on the third Monday of the June term 1826, to answer charges of desertion.

Independent Patriot 22 Apr 1826: 6-23. Jacob W. MILLER vs Mary Ann MILLER- Jacob stated he and Mary Ann were married in March of 1821. He also claimed Mary Ann had left him on March 14, 1824, and was believed to have left the state.

Missouri Intelligencer 14 Dec 1826: 7-25. NOTICE- All persons are cautioned from harbouring, trading, or dealing in any manner with my wife, Rachel WOOD. Levi WOOD, Cooper Co., December 9, 1826.

Missouri Intelligencer 1 Feb 1827: 8-32. NOTICE- Whereas my wife Nancy WINSCOTT, has left my bed and board...Dudley WINSCOTT, January 20, 1827.

Missouri Intelligencer 26 Apr 1827: 8-44. Alzada PHARIS, by her next friend, Jesse CORNELIUS vs Lewis PHARIS- This divorce petition, filed in Howard County during the March term 1827. was published when Lewis was not found in that county.

Missouri Intelligencer 5 July 1827: 9-2. NOTICE- Cynthia ORE has left my bed and board without just cause...Jacob ORE, July 4, 1827.

Missouri Intelligencer 13 Nov 1829: 11-15. NOTICE- Whereas Jane A. HUGHES my wife, left my bed and board on the 5th of October last...John HUGHES, November 7, 1829.

Missouri Intelligencer 11 Dec 1829: 11-19. Eliza YOUNT, by her next friend, Robert BROWN vs George YOUNT- This petition filed in Howard County Circuit Court, stated George was believed to have left the state. He was ordered to appear on the first Monday in March, 1830.

Beacon 27 Jan 1830: 1-69. CAUTION! My Wife Adaline HOBBS, formerly Adaline FAIR, having left my bed and board...Thomas HOBBS.

Beacon 20 Jan 1831: 2-125. NOTICE- Whereas my wife Josette HAMILTON has left without any justifiable cause, left my bed and board...Rich. W. HAMILTON, St. Louis, January 20, 1831.

Beacon 24 Mar 1831: 3-134. CAUTION- Whereas my wife Louisana S. SMART has left my bed and board, disregarding all my solicitations and entreaties... Glover SMART, Callaway Co., March 10, 1831.

Jeffersonian Republican 8 Oct 1831: 5-261. NOTICE- I will pay no debts of my wife Isabel, who has deserted me. Hugh HETHERLY, September 29, 1831.

Beacon 12 Jan 1832: 3-176. NOTICE- Ranaway from my bed and board on the 6th inst. my wife Susan, without my knowledge and against my consent...Alexander COHEN, St. Louis, January 12, 1832.

Beacon 2 Feb 1832: 3-179. NOTICE- This is to forbid all persons dealing with, trusting, or harbouring my wife Emeline T....Wm. McNEIL, St. Louis Arsenal, February 1, 1832.

Beacon 9 Feb 1832: 3-180. NOTICE- Whereas my husband Wm. S. McNEIL has without cause left my bed and board, and has harboured with other women...Emeline T. McNEIL, St. Louis Co., February 3, 1832. The printer will have the goodness to insert this advertisement immediately under that of my husband, and as often as his shall appear (neither notice appeared again).

Missouri Intelligencer 23 Feb 1833: 17-33. NOTICE- Whereas my wife Asseneth has left...and carried off all my goods, household furniture, mare and colt, I am determined to put the law in force. Alfred WINSCOTT.

Missouri Intelligencer 23 Mar 1833: 17-39. NOTICE- My wife Sally STRICKLIN did quit my bed and board in the month of July last...Elcana STRICKLIN, March 18, 1833, St. Louis.

Jeffersonian Republican 21 Dec 1833: 7-344. NOTICE- I will pay no debts of my wife Suzannah, who continues to absent herself without cause, after this date. John PERKIN, December 5, 1833.

Missouri Intelligencer 22 Mar 1834: 17-39. (The following article was condensed from a lengthier piece) Shocking! During the past term of the Lafayette County Court, Leland TROMLEY was put on trial for the murder of one STEVENS. A woman who passed herself off as TROMLEY's wife took the stand in his behalf.

When evidence was entered during the trial, she refused to answer any other questions, and was arrested on a charge of contempt, but was allowed to keep her child with her. After being jailed, she called down to some people in the street and said she had killed her baby. Upon questioning, she claimed she had killed the child because her mother had turned her out and her sister refused to speak to her, and the child's father was about to be hung for murder. Without their help, she had no means of taking care of the child. The Court ordered TROMLEY hung on April 4, 1834.

Missouri Intelligencer 23 Aug 1834: 17-9. Pleasant M. WILLIAMS vs Susan WILLIAMS- Pleasant published his intention to petition the Missouri General Assembly in the November session on the grounds Susan had left him six years earlier for another man.

John RICE vs Elizabeth RICE- This divorce petition was filed with the legislature on the grounds Elizabeth had openly lived with other men.

Shepherd of the Valley 12 Sept 1834: 2-52. NOTICE- My wife Margaret has left my bed and board. Persons trusting her for any amount, do so at their own peril. Charles VACHARD. September 10, 1834.

Shepherd of the Valley 8 Nov 1834: 2-56. NOTICE- Whereas my wife Louise SCHAFFER, formerly Louise LA PRESSE, has left my bed and board...Nicholas SCHAFFER, October 31, 1834.

Missouri Intelligencer 2 May 1835: 17-45. NOTICE...this is to forewarn all persons from trusting or harbouring my wife Martha who has left my bed and board...Ira NASH.

Argus 24 June 1836: 2-10. NOTICE- Whereas my wife Ann KINCAID, alias Ann McKINNOW, has left my bed and board ...P. KINCAID. Franklin County.

Argus 9 Sept 1836: 2-21. NOTICE- Whereas my wife Mildred has left my bed and board...Samuel LEWIS, St. Louis.

Jeffersonian Republican 7 Jan 1837: 10-490. Jane HYATTE, by her next friend, John A. BLAIR vs John H. HYATTE- This petition, filed in Franklin County, claimed Jane and John were married in Lincoln

County, Kentucky in 1833, and they then moved to Missouri. John reportedly left Jane in September of 1834.

Argus 16 Jan 1838: 3-30. Nichibald PRENTICE vs Lucinda PRENTICE- Nichabald stated he married Lucinda JOICE in 1831, in Kentucky before they moved to Missouri. He also claimed Lucinda had deserted him, and their son David, and returned to Kentucky where she was living with another man.

Jeffersonian Republican 26 May 1838: 10-534. Philip HENSON vs Lucinda HENSON- In this petition, filed in Pulaski County, Philip stated he and Lucinda were married in February of 1835, but she left him the following August. Lucinda was ordered to appear on the second Monday in July to answer charges.

Rachel VAUGHAN vs Enoch VAUGHAN- when Rachel filed her petition for divorce, she claimed she and Enoch were married in December of 1834. She accused him of deserting her in March of 1836. He was ordered to appear on the second Monday of July to answer charges.

Jeffersonian Republican 22 Sept 1838: 10-571. Daniel LAKE vs Mary LAKE- Daniel accused Mary of adultery and desertion after she reportedly ran away with William R. HEATH. She was ordered to appear during the December term 1838 before the Benton County Circuit Court.

Jeffersonian Republican 21 Nov 1838: 10-579. TAKE NOTICE- I intend at the present General Assembly of the State of Missouri, on the third Monday of the present month to apply for a divorce from my wife, Elizabeth BAGS, late Elizabeth JOHNSTON. John BAGS.

Argus 29 Mar 1839: 4-49. Francis IMPY vs Rachel IMPY- Francis filed this petition for divorce because his wife refused to come West with him after they were married on October 31, 1834 in Pennsylvania.

Western Emigrant 11 Apr 1839: 1-50. NOTICE- I am ready and willing to find and provide for her (Nancy) in my own house...but if others choose to provide for her elsewhere, they must do so at their own expense. John W. ADAMSON, Georgetown, Pettis Co., Apr. 1, 1839.

Western Emigrant 9 May 1839: 2-2. NOTICE- Whereas my wife Nancy has left my bed and board...John BROWN of Falt Creek, Pettis County, May 9, 1839.

Jeffersonian Republican 17 Aug 1839: 13-597. George GREENWAY vs Frances RUSSELL- In his petition for divorce, George stated he and Frances were married on June 7, 1837. After George fell ill the following August, Frances left him. He later learned she had returned to her other husband. This petition was filed on August 17, 1839 on the grounds of bigamy, and finalized during the March term 1840 in Cole County.

Western Emigrant 26 Sept 1839: 2-22. Charles BUTLER vs Margaret BUTLER- In this petition, filed on September 11, 1839, Charles stated he and Margaret were married in February 1818, but she had left him more two years ago. She was ordered to appear on the fourth Monday of the December term, or the petition would be ordered as a true bill.

Jeffersonian Republican 28 Dec 1839: 13-616. Mary PORTERFIELD vs John N. PORTERFIELD- In her petition for divorce, Mary claimed she and John were married April 10, 1829 in Tennessee. She also stated John left her and their two children in September of 1836. When the petition was filed, Mary and the children had been living in Missouri for over a year. John was ordered to appear on the second Monday of the April term at Mt. Sterling, Gasconade County, to answer the complaint.

Jeffersonian Republican 28 Mar 1840: 13-629. Richard SCAGGS vs Polly SCAGGS- When this divorce petition was filed in Pulaski County, Richard claimed he and Polly were married in July of 1837, but that Polly left the following September. She was ordered to appear the following term to answer the charge of desertion.

Salt River Journal 6 June 1840: 7-35. Leonard HENRY vs Martha Ann HENRY- This petition for divorce was filed in Lincoln County on February 18, 1840. Leonard claimed he and Martha Ann were married on August 27, 1837, but she left with another man on January 30, 1838. Martha Ann was ordered to appear during the August term to answer charges.

Salt River Journal 13 June 1840: 7-35. Elizabeth BENSON, by her next friend, Cornelius HOWARD vs Adam A. BENSON- In her divorce petition, Elizabeth claimed that she and the defendant were married in Warren County in 1830, and the couple moved to St. Louis in 1836. In 1839, Adam took her to her father's, Cornelius Howard, while he went to visit his mother in Georgia. From then until the filing of this petition on May 27, 1840, Elizabeth had not heard from him. Adam was ordered to appear in Warren County Circuit Court to answer charges.

Salt River Journal 19 Sept 1840: 7-49. NOTICE- Whereas my wife Mary has left my bed and board...on Thursday the 8th day of August last...F. WITHINGTON, Lincoln County, Mo.

Boonslick Times 12 Dec 1840: 1-39. NOTICE- Whereas my wife Elizabeth FUGITT has left my bed and board...William FUGITT, Randolph Co.

Salt River Journal 16 Jan 1841: 8-14. Susan Cristy HEISEN, by her next friend, Isreal RULAND vs Ferdinan S. C. HEISEN- In this petition for divorce filed on January 6, 1841 in Lincoln County, Susan claimed she and Ferdinan were married on May 16, 1839. She left him after six weeks, claiming Ferdinan treated her in a cruel and inhuman manner while on drugs. He was ordered to appear on the first Monday of the May term 1841.

Jeffersonian Republican 27 Mar 1841: 13-677. John JACKSON vs Eleanor JACKSON- John stated he and the defendant were married on February 18, 1836 in Illinois when this divorce petition was filed in Gasconade County. Eleanor was ordered to appear during the April term to answer the charge of desertion.

Salt River Journal 29 May 1841: 8-33. NOTICE- This is to forewarn all persons from trading with my wife Elizabeth HARDY as she has absconded from my bed and board. Casper HARDY, May 22, 1841.

Missouri Whig 5 June 1841: 2-44. Euphemia Ann CRAIG vs Samuel T. CRAIG- This divorce petition was filed in Marion County on the grounds of abandonment and because Samuel had been indicted for passing counterfeit money.
    Jane BLINCOE vs Granville BLINCOE- This petition was also filed in Marion County. Claiming they were married in 1837 in Tennessee, Jane stated Granville left her six months later.

Salt River Journal 5 June 1841: 8-34. CAUTION- My wife Mary Ann McCARDIE having left my bed and board with out provocation...James M. McCARDIE.

Salt River Journal 12 June 1841: 8-35. PUBLIC NOTICE- My wife Martha Ann Elizabeth BROWN on the 1st day of June left my bed and board...Geo. W. BROWN.

Jeffersonian Republican 26 June 1841: 14-690. Sarah P. SCOTT, by her next friend, William WYATT vs Thomas SCOTT- This divorce petition was filed in Gasconade County. Sarah claimed that on March 9, 1841 Thomas threatened to kill her before he drove Sarah and their child off the property.

Jeffersonian Republican 17 July 1841: 14-693. Elizabeth TRENT vs Garrett R. TRENT- When this petition for divorce was filed in Kinderhook County (renamed Camden County in 1843), Elizabeth accused Garrett of raping her sister, Amanda BARTLETT, and of murdering her father, William BARTLETT in the fall of 1840. Garrett was ordered to appear on the first Monday of the following term to answer charges.

Nancy SMATHERS vs John SMATHERS- When this petition was filed in Miller County in the March term 1841, Nancy claimed she and the defendant were married in October of 1838. She also stated John left her in July of 1839, and she had not heard from him since.

Salt River Journal 31 July 1841: 8-42. NOTICE- All persons are hereby warned from trading or crediting my wife Lucinda RAY...as she left my bed and board on Friday July 24, 1841. James H. RAY.

Jeffersonian Republican 21 Aug 1841: 14-698. Mary DAVIS vs John DAVIS- Mary filed this petition for divorce in Miller County claiming she and John were married in 1825. She accused him of committing adultery in 1840, and then deserting her.

Salt River Journal 4 Sept 1841: 8-47. NOTICE- All persons are hereby forewarned from trusting my wife Lucy on my account as she has left my bed and board on Wednesday August 11, 1841. James HUGHLETT.

Salt River Journal 23 Oct 1841: 9-2. CAUTION- Circumstances beyond my control, having compelled a separation between my wife, Hannah having mutually agreed to live separate and apart from each other. Wm. SPRATT, Bowling Green, Mo., October 1843.

The Radical 13 Nov 1841: 1-2. NOTICE- My wife Mahala B. HENDRIX having left without just cause...E. HENDRIX, Pike Co.

Missouri Whig 13 Nov 1841: 3-16. Julian NEWCOME vs James NEWCOMB- Claiming she and James were married on June 6, 1837. Julian also stated he left the following August when she filed for divorce in Ralls County. James was ordered to appear on the third Monday of the February term 1842 to answer charges.

Boonslick Times 20 Nov 1841: 2-36. NOTICE- Whereas my wife Lydia HERYFORD has without just cause or provocation left my bed and board...Henry HERYFORD, Chariton County.

The Radical 20 Nov 1841: 1-3. Charles BENNET vs Mary BENNET- The Lincoln County Circuit Court ordered Mary to appear on the third Monday of the March term 1842, after this divorce petition was filed during the October term 1841.

Missouri Whig 25 Dec 1841: 3-22. Hetty C. BAILEY vs William BAILEY- After this petition for divorce was filed in Shelby County, William was ordered to appear on the third day of the next term to answer the charge of desertion.

Margarella DAVIDSON vs William DAVIDSON- This petition was also filed in Shelby County, but William had until the March term to appear.

Boonslick Times 12 Feb 1842: 2-48. Mary Ann GRANT vs William B. GRANT- Mary filed this petition for divorce during the January term 1842 in Randolph County on the grounds William was a habitual drunkard who later deserted her.

Susan WALDEN vs William WALDEN- This petition was filed on the grounds William was guilty of adultery, infamous conduct, and desertion during the January term 1842.

Boonslick Times 19 Feb 1842: 2-49. Ann O. HILBERT vs George HILBERT- George was ordered by the Court to appear on the fourth Monday of the May term 1842, after this petition was filed in Chariton County during the January term 1842.

Jeffersonian Enquirer 31 Mar 1842: 4-1. William MCGEE vs Mary McGEE- When William filed for divorce in Pulaski County in the March term 1842, he claimed he and the defendant were married on January 2, 1838 in Mercer County, Kentucky. He also stated Mary left him on the first day of July of the same year.

NOTICE- Whereas my wife Maria E. HAYS having voluntarily left my bed and board...Levin HAYS, Osage County.

The Radical 2 Apr 1842: 1-22. Henry JUSTICE vs Sophia JUSTICE- This petition was filed in Warren County in March of 1842 on the grounds of desertion. Sophia was ordered to appear on the second Monday of the July term 1842.

Jeffersonian Enquirer 14 Apr 1842: 4-3. CAUTION- Whereas my wife Stacy BOON voluntarily left...I will pay no debt of her contracting from this date. John BOON, Miller County, 7th April 1842.

The Radical 16 Apr 1842: 1-42. Sinar JOHNSTON, by her next friend, A. J. GORDON vs William JOHNSTON- This divorce petition was filed in Lincoln County during the March term 1842. William was ordered to appear on the third Monday of the July term.

Missouri Whig 30 Apr 1842: 3-40. Henrietta SWARTS vs Henry B. SWARTS- After this petition was filed in Scotland County, Henry was ordered to appear during the next term of the Circuit Court.

Missouri Whig 14 May 1842: 3-42. NOTICE- Be it known to all persons that my wife Susan M. TULL did on the fifth day of the present month leave my bed and board...William B. TULL, Marion City, May 10, 1842.

Patriot 29 July 1842: 7-21. NOTICE- Understanding that John C. HANDCOCK is in Iowa territory, and is about to be married to a Lady in that Territory, I take this method of informing her and all who may meet with him that he has a wife now living in Boone County, Mo., (the daughter of Jonathan BARTON). Lerena HANDCOCK, his wife.

Jeffersonian Republican 30 July 1842: 15-737. NOTICE- The public are hereby notified that my wife Emeline S.W. BLAIN has left my bed and board and eloped with another man. Lawson BLAIN, Jefferson City.

Missouri Whig 6 Aug 1842: 4-2. NOTICE- Whereas my wife Margaret ROBERTS has left my bed and board... Benjamin ROBERTS.

The Radical 27 Aug 1842: 1-43. NOTICE- whereas my wife Nancy TUTT having left my house without just cause...B. G. TUTT, August 20, 1842.

Boonslick Times 7 Sept 1842: 3-27. Mary TOUT vs Charles TOUT- After this divorce petition was filed in Macon County during the August term 1842, Charles was ordered to appear December 29, 1842 to answer charges of desertion.

The Radical 10 Sept 1842: 1-45. Hendley K. HUTCHINSON vs Louisa V. HUTCHINSON- Hendley published a notice that his divorce was granted by the Pike County Circuit Court.

Jeffersonian Republican 8 Oct 1842: 15-747. Mary J. JAMES vs George JAMES- This petition for divorce was filed in Cole County.

The Radical 14 Jan 1843: 2-11. NOTICE- My wife Elizabeth S. SEELYE having left my bed and board... George SEELYE.

Boonslick Times 11 Feb 1843: 3-48. Elizabeth DEVINY vs Jonathan M. DEVINY- This divorce petition was filed during the December term 1842 on the grounds Jonathan had been gone for more than two years.

Jeffersonian Enquirer 11 May 1843: 5-7. NOTICE- This is to forewarn the public that my wife Martha C. HENDERSON having left my bed and board...John H. HENDERSON.

Jeffersonian Enquirer 8 June 1843: 5-11. CAUTION- Whereas my wife Mary S. JAMES has left...I will pay no debts of her contracting after this date. G. W. JAMES, June 8, 1843.

Boonslick Times 24 June 1843: NOTICE- The conduct of my wife Edith P. ALEXANDER being such as to render my condition intolerable, I have taken steps to divorce myself from the bonds of matrimony. Reuben ALEXANDER.

Hamon MILLION vs Eliza MILLION- When he filed his petition for divorce in May of 1843 in Howard County, Hamon claimed to have married Eliza on January 1, 1837, but that she left him on November of 1838.

Missouri Register 26 Sept 1843: 5-12. ELOPEMENT- Left my bed and board without just cause or provocation my wife Sarah...W. LAURIE, Morgan Co., August 8, 1843.

The Radical 30 Sept 1843: 2-48. CAUTION- The undersigned having for good and sufficient cause, separated from his wife Elvira and intending to make ample provisions for her...Tyree MARTIN.

Jeffersonian Enquirer 2 Nov 1843: 5-31. NOTICE- Whereas my wife, Sophia...left my house on Sunday the 15th instant. Ferdinand REUSELBACH. Cole County.

Jeffersonian Enquirer 9 Nov 1843: 5-32. NOTICE- Whereas my wife Elizabeth Margaret WILLIG formerly Margaret WOLFRAMP has left my bed and board...Henry L. WILLIG.

Jeffersonian Republican 25 Nov 1843: 15-770. Celia BURRUS, alias Celia A. BRIST vs Levi J. BIRST- Celia filed her petition for divorce on the grounds of cruel and intolerable treatment in Cole County.

The Radical 2 Dec 1843: 3-5. Asariah PELLIT vs Julia Ann PELLIT, alias Julia Ann LANDON- Asariah filed this divorce petition with the help of his solicitor, A. H. BUCKNER during the October term 1843. Julia was ordered to appear on the second Monday of the April term 1843 to answer the charges.

Sarah HAGOOD, by her next friend, Richard ESTIS vs James A. HAGOOD- This petition was filed in Lincoln County during the November term 1843. James was to appear on the first Monday of the May term 1843.

John BELLMEYER vs Rebecca BELLMEYER- Filed during the October term 1843 in Pike County on the grounds of desertion, this petition was heard by the Circuit Court which then ordered Rebecca to appear on the second Monday in April of 1844.

Weekly Observer 17 Apr 1844: 5-6. Nancy M. TAYLOR vs William H. TAYLOR- This divorce petition was filed in Cooper County. William was ordered to appear on the second Monday of the September term.

Boonslick Times 2 Mar 1844: 4-51. Melissa MYERS vs George MYERS- Melissa filed this divorce petition during the December term 1843. She claimed that she and the defendant were married May 24, 1831. She also stated George deserted their family on September 20, 1839. Melissa requested the Court grant her custody and control of their two sons and general relief.

Boonslick Times 4 May 1844: 5-8. Ann Eliza KEISTER vs Washington KEISTER- This petition was filed by Ann's solicitor, Joseph FISK, on April 20, 1844 in Chariton County. Ann claimed she and Washington were married on February 6, 1841, but after that he began to accuse her of adultery. He finally left on January 10, 1843. Ann requested the Court grant her alimony.

Springfield Advertiser 28 May 1844: 1-3. NOTICE- This is to forewarn the public from trusting my wife Margaret Ann on my account as I will pay no debts of her contracting...Garrick W. AKIN.

Missouri Register 16 July 1844: 5-42. NOTICE- In as much as my wife Catherine KENNEBLY has left...I deem it well to add that she is the third of her mother's children who has left her family viz: two sons and one daughter. Shelton KENNEBLY, Cooper Co., July 12, 1844.

Springfield Advertiser 23 July 1844: 1-11. Flora S. EMMONS vs Ira EMMONS- This petition was filed on the grounds of desertion, and Ira was ordered to appear the following term to answer charges.

Springfield Advertiser 20 Aug 1844: 1-15. Savil GUNNER vs Mary GUNNER- When Savil filed his petition for divorce in Barry County, he claimed his wife had been a habitual drunkard for more than two years. She was ordered to appear on the fourth Monday of the November term 1844, or the petition would be entered into record as a true bill.
Jane M. HARPER, by her next friend J. M. DONNELL vs Robert HARPER- When Jane filed this petition for divorce in Greene County Circuit Court she requested custody of the couple's two children.

Missouri Register 17 Sept 1844: 5-50. TO THE PUBLIC- Whereas my wife Ann P. TUCKER has left my house and abandoned me and my children...James TUCKER.

Springfield Advertiser 17 Dec 1844: 1-31. Emilia LEDFORD vs John LEDFORD- Emelia stated she and the defendant were married in 1839, when she filed for divorce in Jasper County. She also claimed John left her in September of 1842.

Springfield Advertiser 31 Dec 1844: 1-33. Stephen D. SUTTON vs Susannah SUTTON- When this petition for divorce was filed in Barry County, Stephen claimed he had married Susannah in 1831 in Jackson County, Alabama, but it was not until 1833 that she left him. Susannah was ordered to appear in Circuit Court on the fourth Monday of the April term 1845 to answer charges.

Lexington Express 7 Jan 1845: 5-31. Joan PARKER vs Thomas F. PARKER- This petition for divorce was filed in Andrew County Circuit Court. At that time, Joan claimed she and the defendant were married in February of 1841 in Johnson County, but Thomas left in August of 1842. He was ordered to appear during the March term.

Missouri Whig 8 Jan 1845: 6-25. Henry PEMBERTON vs Jane PEMBERTON- Henry was represented by his solicitor, C. F. KIRT-LEY, when he filed for a divorce in Marion County, claiming Jane had left him in 1821. She was ordered to appear in Court on the second Monday of the April term.

Springfield Advertiser 28 Jan 1845: 1-37. James M. HOUSE vs Louisa HOUSE- This petition was filed by James' solicitor, Edward

M. HOLDEN, in Ripley County. Louisa was ordered to appear on the fourth Monday of the April term to answer the charge of desertion.

St. Joseph Gazette 23 May 1845: 1-5. Frederick ARRENT vs Sarah ARRENT- This petition for divorce was filed in Andrew County in March of 1845. Sarah was to appear on September 15, 1845 to answer charges.

Sarah Ann RECTOR vs Nelson RECTOR- This divorce petition was filed in Buchanan County, and Nelson was ordered to appear on the fourth Monday in September of 1845.

John HARTMAN vs Eliza HARTMAN- When this petition for divorce was filed in September of 1844 in Andrew County, John stated he and Eliza were married in January of 1839. She was ordered to appear on September 15, 1845 to answer the complaint.

St. Joseph Gazette 30 May 1845: 1-6. Susannah MILLER vs Samuel MILLER- This petition for divorce was filed in Andrew County in March of 1845 on the grounds Samuel had treated Susannah in a cruel and barbarous manner.

Lexington Express 17 July 1845: 6-2. Ann EDMUNSON vs Isaac EDMUNSON- Ann filed for divorce in Van Buren County (now Cass County) on the grounds of desertion. In her petition she claimed she and Isaac were married on July 15, 1837 in Tennessee, and that they moved to Missouri in 1839. Isaac reportedly left her in 1841.

St. Joseph Gazette 27 June 1845: 1-16. Rebecca Maria WHITLOW vs Hiram WHITLOW- After this divorce petition was filed in Buchanan County, the Court ordered Hiram to appear and answer charges on the fourth Monday in September of 1845.

Springfield Advertiser 28 June 1845: 2-5. John ALLEN vs Letta ALLEN- This petition was filed in Taney County in May of 1845 on the grounds of desertion. Letta was to appear on the fourth Monday of the next term.

Springfield Advertiser 5 July 1845: 2-6. Melcena A. HAMMOND, by her solicitor J. E. GARY vs Jerome G. HAMMOND- When this petition was filed in Greene County on June 30, 1845, Melcena asked for custody of her and Jerome's child.

Springfield Advertiser 12 July 1845: 2-7. James THOMPSON vs Winney THOMPSON- This petition for divorce was filed during the May term 1845 in Taney County on the grounds of adultery and desertion.

Springfield Advertiser 2 Aug 1845: 2-10. Ellen OVERTON vs Edmund OVERTON- This divorce petition was filed on July 29, 1845 on the grounds of desertion. Edmund was ordered to appear in Court on the fourth Monday in October.

Springfield Advertiser 9 Aug 1845: 2-11. Nancy Ann GIBSON vs John GIBSON- Nancy accused John of barbaric and cruel treatment when she filed her petition for divorce in Pulaski County.

Mary Ann MORGAN vs Reuben B. MORGAN- When this petition was filed in Pulaski County, the Court ordered Reuben to appear on the third day of the next term to answer charges.

Elizabeth TENISON vs Harrison TENISON- This petition was also filed in Pulaski on the grounds of desertion, but Harrison was ordered to appear on the fourth Monday of the October term.

Weekly Reveille 19 Aug 1845: 2-394. Mary DELILE vs Alexander DELILE- After Mary filed for divorce in St. Louis County, Alexander was ordered to appear on the third Monday of the November term.

Jeffersonian Enquirer 11 Sept 1845: 7-24. NOTICE- Is hereby given to all persons that I have once before this given notice in the public paper of the separation of myself and wife, and that she has gone off again without just cause. Charles EGGERS, Cole County, Mo.

NOTICE- Whereas my wife Catherine, left my bed and board on the 13th of the present month...Charles FRISCH, Cole County.

Missouri Whig 24 Sept 1845: 7-10. NOTICE- Whereas my wife Elizabeth LEGG has left my bed and board...Robert LEGG, Lagrange, September 23, 1845.

Missouri Whig 20 Nov 1845: 7-18. Sarah Ann SLODERBACK, by her next friend Granville R. MILL vs John SLODERBACK- In her petition for divorce, Sarah told the Marion County Circuit Court that she was the former Sarah Ann MILLER. John was ordered by the Court to appear on the first Monday of the March term to answer the charge of desertion.

Springfield Advertiser 29 Nov 1845: 2-27. NOTICE is hereby given that my wife Susanna Jane BLACK did on the 16th of this·month leave my house and home... Jeremiah BLACK, Polk County, November 17, 1845.

Herald of Religious Liberty 1 Jan 1846: 2-26. Elizabeth FOREMAN vs Joseph FOREMAN- Filed in Franklin County, this divorce petition was published along with an order for Joseph to appear on the first Monday of the March term.

Springfield Advertiser 10 Jan 1846: 2-27. Garrick W. AKIN vs Margaret AKIN- This divorce petition was filed in Greene County on December 12, 1845. Margaret was to appear during the April term.

Springfield Advertiser 30 May 1846: 3-1. Elizabeth HALEY vs Isaac HALEY- After this petition for divorce was filed in Dallas County, the Court ordered Isaac to appear on the third Monday in September.

Springfield Advertiser 13 June 1846: 3-3. Nancy M. ELLINGTON vs Daniel ELLINGTON- This divorce petition was filed in Greene County on June 3, 1846, but Daniel had until the October term to answer charges.

Springfield Advertiser 18 July 1846: 3-8. William B. BOYD vs Hulda Maria BOYD- William filed this divorce petition on July 9, 1846 in Greene County. Huldah was ordered to appear during the October term to answer the charge of desertion.

St. Louis Daily Union 17 Aug 1846: 1-1. Jane EVANS, formerly Jane ROSS vs Lambert EVANS- This petition was filed in St. Louis County on the grounds of desertion.

St. Joseph Gazette 4 Dec 1846: 2-99. David STOUT vs Rebecca STOUT- When this divorce petition was filed in Nodaway County, David told the Court he and the defendant were married in March of 1841, and she had been gone more than two years. Rebecca was to appear in Court on March 8, 1847.

The Metropolitan 21 Dec 1847: 2-12. Nancy REINHART vs Davis W. REINHART- This petition was filed in Cole County during the November term 1847, on the grounds of desertion.
    Elizabeth LOGAN vs William LOGAN- This divorce petition was also filed in Cole County.

St. Joseph Gazette 14 Jan 1848: 3-20. Nancy LUCAS vs Joseph LUCAS- After this petition for divorce was filed in Buchanan County on October 6, 1846, Joseph was ordered to appear on the first Monday of the March term.
    Mozella LYNCH vs Alvis LYNCH- This petition was published by order of the Buchanan County Circuit Court.

Platte Argus 14 June 1848: 4-36. Joseph S. SNIDER vs Elizabeth SNIDER- In this petition for divorce, filed in Platte County on October 8, 1847, Joseph told the Court he and the defendant were married in 1813 in Rockingham County, Virginia.

Springfield Advertiser 10 Mar 1848: 3-28. NOTICE- As my wife, Catherine NOBLE, wife of the undersigned having abandoned his bed and board...William NOBLE, March 1, 1848.

Platte Argus 9 June 1848: 5-5. Melvira DRYDEN vs Samuel DRYDEN- In her petition for divorce, Melvira declared she and Samuel were married on December 22, 1842, and that he left her on January 2, 1844. An affidavit by Pleasant ELLINGTON declared Samuel was not a resident of the county, so the Court ordered the publication of the petition.

Missouri Whig 9 Nov 1848: 10-17. Ellen CURTIS vs Charles H. CURTIS- This petition for divorce, filed by the former Ellen GRUNDY MULDROW, and her agent, James F. MAHAN in Marion County, ordered Charles to appear anytime from the first to the sixth day of the March term.

Missouri Whig 16 Nov 1848: 10-18. Asel COLEMAN vs Lockey Jane COLEMAN- This petition filed in Marion County, ordered Lockey to appear by the sixth day of the March term.

The Fulton Telegraph 1 Dec 1848: 4-21. Margaret E. BROWN vs Samuel BROWN- This petition for divorce was filed in Callaway County on October 13, 1848 on the grounds of desertion.
NOTICE- My husband Joseph P. BOULDIN left me and took my two children Mary Ellen and John William. Mary Ellen was 5 years old on the 11th of June last and John was 3 years old on the 3rd of September and he also took with him my sister Mary Lee and I suppose they will pass as man and wife. $100 reward paid to anyone who will return my children or tell me where I can find them. The said Joseph is about 5 feet 7 inches with a fair complexion and brown hair. Mary Lee is a heavy built woman with a fair complexion and sandy hair...Susan BOULDIN, Piqua, Ohio, July 1, 1848.
Francis A. DRILLER vs Caroline DRILLER- This petition for divorce was filed in Carroll County. Martin was ordered to appear on the second Monday of the March term to answer the charge of abandonment.

Canton Plebeian 19 Jan 1849: 1-31. Sarah BOATRIGHT vs John BOATRIGHT- Filed in Clark County in October of 1848, this petition stated the couple was married in 1844. It was also claimed that John left in the spring of 1846.

The Fulton Telegraph 19 Jan 1849: 4-28. Emmely GRIGGS vs Shelton GRIGGS- This divorce petition was filed in Montgomery County on January 5, 1849.

Missouri Whig 16 Aug 1849: 11-15. NOTICE- I hereby notify the public that my wife Catherine H. RUTTER has left my premises against my consent...Chambers RUTTER, July 2, 1849.

The Fulton Telegraph 17 Aug 1849: 5-6. NOTICE is hereby given that my wife Sally WALTON left my bed and board on the 4th inst....Thompson WALTON.

The Fulton Telegraph 26 Oct 1849: 5-15. NOTICE- Whereas my wife Mary A. DAY has left my bed and board...William T. DAY.

The Fulton Telegraph 9 Nov 1849; 5-17. Margaret L. DAVIDSON vs James DAVIDSON- This petition was filed in the Montgomery County Circuit Court during the September term 1849.

Missouri Republican 22 Jan 1850: 29-19. Henry FARMER vs Harriet FARMER- Henry filed for divorce in St. Louis County on December 18, 1849. Harriet was required to appear in Court on the third Monday of the April term 1850, to answer the charge of desertion.

RECORDS OF BIGAMY CASES
1819 - 1845

State of Missouri vs Martin SCHOLL- Indicted for bigamy on March 28, 1821 in New Madrid Co. Charges were dropped July 25, 1821.

State of Missouri vs Nancy BUSEY, alias Nancy WOOD- Indicted for bigamy during the February term 1845 in Holt County.

State of Missouri vs Peter FOX- Peter was indicted for bigamy in Chariton County in October of 1845.

State of Missouri vs Waller H. MIBHAUR- Indicted for bigamy on July 13, 1843 in Platte County.

State of Missouri vs James J. TUCKER- Indicted for bigamy in Polk County, but in June of 1843 the Circuit Court attorney stated he would not continue to prosecute the case.

United States vs Thomas WILLBURN- Indicted for bigamy in the New Madrid district on April 14, 1819.

State of Missouri vs Elizabeth MITCHER- This bigamy suit went to trial in Macon County during the August term 1841.

State of Missouri vs Solomon FISHER- Indicted for bigamy, Samuel plead not guilty in Pike County on May 28, 1832. In the first trial, the jury could not agree on a verdict. The second jury moved to drop the case when a material witness, Robert A. STARK failed to appear. Samuel was found not guilty on May 29, 1833, and Robert STARK was charged with contempt.

During the March term 1824, the Cooper County Circuit Court handed down indictments against two men, Ezekiel WILLIAMS and Elisha SPIRA for bigamy.

State of Missouri vs Susan BISHOP, alias Susan ROARK- Susan was found guilty of bigamy during the July term 1823 in Franklin County.

INDEX

AARON, 58
ABERNATHY, 19
ABLE, 2
ABRAMS, 39
ADAMS, 57
ADAMSON, 68
AIGUIES, 48
AIKEN, 3
AKIN, 75 79
ALEXANDER, 74
ALFREY, 11
ALIDAR, 59
ALIDER, 59
ALLEN, 46 52 77
AMBROSE, 61
ANDERSON, 16
ANDREWS, 4
APPLEGATE, 9
ARMFIELD, 41
ARMSTRONG, 47 59
ARNST, 55
ARRENT, 24 38 77
ATTERBARY, 61
ATTERBURY, 39
AUBIN, 18
AUBUCHUM, 59
AUSTIN, 27 36
BAGS, 68
BAILEY, 72
BAKER, 4 28
BALLENTINE, 59
BAMPENDAHL, 54
BANISTER, 47
BARKER, 7
BARNES, 8
BARTLETT, 71

BARTON, 73
BATTLEBY, 57
BAY, 58
BAYER, 7
BEAUCHAMP, 31
BEAVERS, 27
BECKER, 55
BEESON, 56
BELCHER, 9
BELLESIME, 27 29
BELLMEYER, 75
BENNET, 72
BENSON, 69
BENT, 9
BENTON, 46
BEST, 12
BESWELL, 10
BEVERADGE, 53
BEYON, 45
BIRCH, 12
BIRST, 75
BISHOP, 83
BLACK, 78
BLACKBURN, 2
BLAIN, 73
BLAINE, 32
BLAIR, 2 67
BLANY, 52
BLINCOE, 70
BOATRIGHT, 80
BOLGIANO, 49 52
BOOKER, 18
BOON, 73
BOOTH, 58
BOTTS, 35
BOULDIN, 81

86

DARGE, 53
DARNALL, 19
DAUGHTERS, 9
DAVIDSON, 16 51 72 81
DAVIS, 2 3 18 40 52 58 61 71
DAWSON, 59
DAY, 81
DEBBIN, 30
DEHODIAMONT, 51
DEJARDIN, 33
DELEY, 3
DELILE, 78
DEPRE, 39
DEROIN, 30 32
DETAILLE, 49
DEVINY, 74
DEWITT, 27
DODD, 17
DODGE, 28
DODIER, 32
DONNELL, 76
DOOLIN, 40
DOWLING, 47
DRENAN, 47
DRILLER, 80
DRYDEN, 80
DUBAI, 28
DUCHOQUETTE, 54
DUMAS, 14
DUNCAN, 21 43
DUNKLIN, 2
DUNN, 6 64
EADS, 2 3
EASTON, 5 46
EATON, 45
ECKLER, 42
EDDS, 30 32
EDISON, 10
EDMUNDSON, 23
EDMUNSON, 77
EDSON, 45
EGGERS, 78
ELDER, 49
ELLINGTON, 79 80
ELLIOT, 43

ELLSTON, 59
ELLSWORTH, 56
EMMONS, 76
ENOS, 45
EPPERSON, 37
ESTIS, 75
EVANS, 79
FAIR, 66
FANNING, 7
FAREWELL, 62
FAREWILL, 62
FARMER, 81
FAWKES, 40
FERGUSON, 42
FISHBACK, 3
FISHER, 83
FISK, 75
FLETCHER, 20 48 50 58
FLOREZ, 55
FOLEY, 13
FORBES, 24
FORBIS, 24
FOREMAN, 78
FOREST, 7
FORESTER, 32
FOSTER, 5 63
FOURTER, 14
FOWLER, 15 37
FOX, 83
FRANKLIN, 10 40
FRAZER, 6
FRISCH, 78
FRY, 42
FUCHS, 57
FUGATE, 58
FUGITT, 70
GAINES, 1
GARBER, 8
GARNER, 45
GARRET, 52
GATES, 3
GATSON, 13
GAY, 49
GEISLER, 59
GENTRY, 13 42

GIBBS, 19
GIBONEY, 3
GIBSON, 6 18 38 40 78
GIGUANE, 61
GILBERT, 2 5
GILL, 57
GILLIS, 30
GILLMAN, 56
GILSTRAP, 21
GINGRA, 53
GLASCOCK, 12
GLASS, 28
GLOSCLAUDE, 53
GOALD, 63
GOETZ, 25
GOLDSMITH, 57
GORIN, 40
GORDON, 73
GRAHAM, 55
GRANJEAN, 49
GRANT, 72
GRAVES, 3
GREEN, 3 40
GREENWAY, 69
GREGORY, 52
GRIFFAR, 64
GRIFFEN, 5
GRIFFITH, 59
GRIGGS, 81
GRIST, 32
GRUNDY, 80
GUERRANT, 10
GUM, 14
GUNNER, 76
HAGEN, 13 62
HAGGERTY, 62
HAGOOD, 75
HAILE, 2
HALEY, 79
HALL, 46
HAMILTON, 35 51 66
HAMMOND, 77
HANDCOCK, 73
HANNAH, 1
HARDING, 10

HARDY, 70
HARGIS, 42
HARPER, 76
HARRINGTON, 11 14
HARRIS, 36 41 50
HART, 32
HARTMAN, 21 77
HARVEY, 36
HAWKE, 39
HAWKINS, 12 37
HAYDEN, 13
HAYS, 72
HEATH, 68
HEISEN, 70
HENDERSON, 74
HENDRICK, 46
HENDRIX, 71
HENRY, 48 69
HENSLEY, 50
HENSON, 68
HEREFORD, 19 36
HERRIMAN, 42
HERYFORD, 72
HETHERLY, 66
HEWS, 65
HIBLER, 46 48
HICKMAN, 53
HIGGENBOTHAM, 52
HIGH, 39
HILBERT, 72
HILL, 3 11 39 40 55
HINEMAN, 39
HINKS, 1
HINSON, 5 64
HOBBS, 66
HODGES, 11
HOGAN, 24 62
HOHNHOLIZ, 55
HOLDEN, 77
HOLDERMAN, 23 53
HOLIDAY, 19
HOPE, 14
HORINE, 23
HORITZ, 29
HORO, 7

NOWLIN, 35
NUNNELLY, 58
NUTT, 40
O'BRYAN, 43
OBUCHON, 52
ODELL, 39
OGLESBY, 52
ORE, 65
ORNOOCE, 32
ORR, 9
OVERTON, 78
OWEN, 22
OWENS, 5 37 64
OWNEY, 36
PACKWOOD, 20
PAGE, 41
PAGET, 28
PAINE, 46
PALMER, 13
PAPEN, 39
PARKER, 24 76
PATERSON, 31
PATTERSON, 3 27 61
PATTON, 5 64
PAULET, 32
PAYNE, 41
PAYTON, 39
PEARSON, 46
PELLIT, 75
PEMBERTON, 39 76
PENNY, 11
PEPPER, 9 65
PERKIN, 66
PERKINS, 40
PETTIT, 2
PHARIS, 65
PHELAN, 46
PHILLEBAR, 25
PIBEN, 3
PILE, 41
POOL, 15
PORE, 18
PORTER, 31 56
PORTERFIELD, 16 69
POWELL, 25

PRENTICE, 68
PRIGHT, 2
PROBST, 12
PROUIX, 29
PRUETT, 29
PULLAM, 65
PURSELL, 31
RAFFERTY, 51
RANCONTRE, 30
RANNEY, 3
RAWLINGS, 58
RAY, 71
RAYBURN, 23
RECTOR, 77
REDDING, 22
REDMAN, 15
REED, 36
REGNIER, 1 30
REINHART, 35 41 79
REMICK, 11
RENNOLDS, 57
REUSELBACH, 74
REYNOLDS, 12 24 42
RICE, 67
RICHARD, 29 51
RICHARDS, 35
RIDDLE, 54
RIDGEWAY, 40
RIGHT, 4
ROARK, 83
ROBERTS, 63 73
ROBIN, 27
ROBINSON, 32
ROCKHOLD, 11
RODNEY, 4
ROGUS, 25
ROLAND, 41
ROOF, 16
ROOK, 17
ROP, 37
ROUNCE, 15
ROUNDTREE, 56
ROUTH, 40
ROY, 30
RUBEY, 36

VALL, 3
VALLE, 1 27 30
VANDERFORD, 16
VANDUZEN, 19
VAN GRAILMAN, 38
VAUGHAN, 68
VIATELL, 41
VISTAL, 22
WALDEN, 72
WALDS, 9
WALL, 61
WALLACE, 37
WALLITE, 56
WALTON, 81
WARDEN, 38
WASH, 37
WATLENS, 12
WATSON, 5 6
WATT, 39
WEATHERS, 2
WEBB, 56
WEIR, 17
WELCH, 29 46
WELDON, 36
WELLS, 16 20 46
WEST, 28
WESTOVER, 11
WHEELER, 19
WHILTEY, 29
WHITE, 22 54

WHITLOW, 3 77
WICE, 16
WICKS, 31
WILLBURN, 83
WILLIAMS, 7 13 63 64 67 83
WILLIG, 74
WILLIS, 50
WILLS, 62
WILSON, 20 39
WINCHESTER, 22 55
WINDER, 63
WINDES, 5
WINES, 33
WINSCOTT, 65 66
WINTER, 14
WITHINGTON, 70
WITT, 13
WOLFRAMP, 74
WOOD, 3 65 83
WOODARD, 7
WOODBRIDGE, 9 48
WRIGHT, 55
WYATT, 71
WYRICK, 25
YARNELL, 61
YORK, 13
YOUNG, 10 16
YOUNT, 36 65
ZUMWALT, 8 37